THE LITTLE BOOK OF

FITNESS LAW

CECIL C. KUHNE III

AMERICAN BAR ASSOCIATION
Defending Liberty
Pursuing Justice

Cover design by Andrew Alcala/ABA Publishing.

Printed in the United States of America.

18 17 16 15 14 5 4 3 2 1

Library of Congress Cataloging-in-Publication Data

Kuhne, Cecil C., III, 1952-
  The little book of fitness law / by Cecil Kuhne.
    pages cm
  Includes bibliographical references and index.
  ISBN 978-1-62722-478-9 (alk. paper)
  1. Physical fitness centers--Law and legislation--United States--Cases. 2. Sports--Law and legislation--United States--Cases. 3. Liability for sports accidents--United States--Cases. I. Title.
  KF2042.P49K84 2014
  344.73'099--dc23
                    2014004290

www.ShopABA.org

Table of Contents

When I feel like exercising, I just lie down until the feeling goes away.

Robert M. Hutchins

I have to exercise in the morning before my brain figures out what I'm doing.

Marsha Doble

THE LITTLE BOOK OF

FITNESS LAW

Introduction

Perhaps the only thing more dangerous than being *out* of shape is trying to get *in* shape.

The misery begins, of course, with those dreaded exercise machines, which in an earlier day were called *medieval torture devices*. From them emanates the excruciating pain of pounding into submission underutilized, citified muscles. And then comes the inevitable soreness of stretching into positions that the human body was really never meant to be stretched into. It makes me tired just to think about it all.

But fortunately, these efforts sometimes pay off. Look around your health club. A friend of mine, surveying the fit patrons in his gym, put it this way: "These people have muscles in places that I don't even *have* places."

Luckily for the trial bar, the mad rush—by hoards of somewhat pudgy people in a hurry to look good for the upcoming swimsuit season—has led to a healthy amount of litigation (some of it rather intriguing), such as the following:

- Yoko Zipusch was exercising at LA Workout when her foot "allegedly" became stuck to a nondescript substance on the belt of the treadmill she was plying. This resulted in Yoko losing her balance, which caused her to be hurled off the whirling dervish of a device. Yoko filed suit against the club for failure to inspect and properly maintain its equipment.
- Pritikin Longevity Center and Spa is a tony health club ensconced within the confines of the Santa Monica Beach Hotel. As was his custom, Tom Benedek was about to use an elliptical training machine that faced a large television suspended high above. When he tried to reposition the set, it started to slide off the rack. Benedek courageously tried to stop its momentum, but he badly injured himself in the process.

- A member of the Narragansett Tennis Club, Carol Hueston, suffered a severe avulsion of the finger when she tried to retrieve a tennis ball. On occasion, tennis balls would become lodged in the channel formed by the horizontal wall girders, and Carol's ring caught on the metal lip as she reached inside to rescue the errant ball.

- The competition for those who buy athletic swimsuits can be intense. To assist in the promotion of its swimwear line, Speedo hired the head coach of USA Swimming, the national governing body. Another swimsuit manufacturer, TYR Sport, complained about the coach's claim that a Speedo suit, the LZR Racer, provided a "two percent advantage" over the others. USA Swimming was also accused of altering photographs of swimmers to remove logos of competitors, and of conspiring to prevent advertising of other swimsuit companies in the official magazine.

- Alfred Sicard was a scholarship player on the University of Dayton's basketball team, and he was told to lift weights in order to improve his fitness. Sicard claimed that Dave Bollwinkel, a university employee, agreed to act as a spotter while Sicard lifted a 365-pound barbell. Sicard's strength failed him, and two other spotters were unable to stop the falling weight. Bollwinkel had apparently turned away to speak to someone else, and offered no assistance. Sicard suffered a ruptured pectoral muscle, and he sued the university and Bollwinkel for his harm.

- A fraternity party was held at Abbey Racquetball Club, where the rental agreement explicitly required (a) the presence of five adult chaperones, and (b) the understanding that *absolutely* "no physical fitness equipment may be used." Nevertheless, during the party, one of the attendees, Ilene Forgang, decided to use the "pec dec" chest-press machine.

Soon after she sat down, she was forcefully struck on both sides of her face by the arms of the machine. Ilene's workout session was very brief, but her injuries were not.

- One fine April day, Robert McGuire was jogging on Palm Drive in New Orleans City Park near one of its golf courses. As he crossed the bridge near Hole No. 3, a golf ball bounced on the road in front of him and then forcefully struck him in the groin. Robert sued the operator of the golf course, alleging that it had breached its duties to (a) warn of the danger of flying golf balls, and (b) configure the course to reduce the danger to runners.

- Artist Michael Stanard designed and sold t-shirts and sweatshirts with the Nike "swoosh," but with the word "Mike" instead of "Nike." Apparently, the company saw no humor in the imitation, and it sued for trademark infringement. Stanard responded with a parody defense, claiming the word play deserved First Amendment protection as "fair use."

- Michael Pappalardo, a member of The New York Health & Racquet Club, was using a "leg curl" machine on the second floor. After completing a set of repetitions, he stepped aside so his friend could begin exercising. Michael was near the window, and while bending over to tie his shoe, the glass behind him shattered and he fell ten feet to the pavement below. Fortunately, he lived to tell about it.

And there are many more equally fascinating cases dealing with the world of fitness litigation—traffic citations for running in the nude, Ironman triathlons, intellectual disputes over energy drinks, miniature fitness trampolines, bicycle safety, backyard basketball, obsessive-compulsive joggers, the obligation of a health club to provide CPR, and open drain holes that joggers accidentally fall into, to name but a few. The book will take a look at the wide spectrum of knotty legal disputes arising from the physical fitness arena, and the courts' erstwhile efforts to mend fences and compensate victims.

In the end, as diverse as these stories are, they do seem to have one thing in common—they reveal that working out can sometimes be extremely hazardous to one's health.

The Health Club

Chapter 1

Treacherous Treadmill: The Duty to Inspect Equipment

Zipusch v. LA Workout, 155 Cal. App. 4th 1281 (2007)

Treadmills can be deceptively dangerous devices. Just ask Yoko Zipusch.

Zipusch allegedly sustained injuries when her foot somehow became "mysteriously" stuck to an unknown substance on a treadmill, causing her to stumble badly and then fall off the unrelenting machine. Zipusch filed suit against her beloved health club, LA Workout, for general negligence and premises liability, alleging that its failure to rigorously inspect and maintain its exercise equipment was the direct cause of her injuries.

When she first joined the health club, Zipusch (like everyone else) signed a lengthy membership agreement containing provisions for assumption of the risk, release of liability, and indemnification:

> The use of the facility at LA Workout naturally involves the
> risk of injury. As such you understand and voluntarily accept

this risk and agree that LA Workout will not be liable for injury, including without limitation, personal, bodily, or mental injury, economic loss, or damage. If there is any claim by anyone based on injury, loss, or damage, you agree to (1) defend LA Workout against such claims and pay LA Workout for all expenses relating to the claim, and (2) indemnify LA Workout for all liabilities to you, your spouse, guests, relatives, or anyone else, resulting from such claims. The member or guest will defend and indemnify LA Workout for any negligence EXCEPT the sole negligence of the club.

In its motion for summary judgment, LA Workout urged the court to find that these provisions released the athletic club from *all* claims arising from a member's use of the facilities. Zipusch naturally opposed the motion, contending that the release *only* barred claims caused by negligent third-party conduct, and alternatively, that the release contained an ambiguity, which should be construed against the drafter. Either way, Zipusch maintained that the release did *not* bar claims against the health club for its *own* negligence in maintaining and inspecting the equipment.

Zipusch presented detailed evidence to prove her allegations. Zipusch claimed, first of all, that eighty-five minutes elapsed between the time of the accident and the last time a gym employee had inspected and cleaned the equipment. Secondly, an assistant manager of the health club testified that the undersides of treadmill belts were *never* routinely inspected. Zipusch contended that a reasonable trier of fact could find that this was negligent conduct.

In spite of these seemingly persuasive arguments, the trial court granted summary judgment in favor of LA Workout based upon the assumption of risk provision. The court found that while the release did not bar *all* claims arising from use of the health club, it did bar all claims involving *third-party* conduct. In this regard, the trial court pointed out that Zipusch presented *no* evidence indicating that the substance was placed on the treadmill by the health club itself.

Zipusch appealed, contending there still remained issues of material fact regarding two matters: whether the liability release exculpated the health club from its own negligence, and whether the health club negligently failed to inspect and clean its equipment.

Assumption of Risk Provision

The appellate court, it turned out, agreed with Zipusch. In its analysis of the membership agreement, the assumption of risk provision contemplated two types of potential injuries: injuries to a member caused by others, and injuries to others caused by a member. Significant in the court's mind was the fact that the clause began with an introductory sentence warning about the *inherent* risks of using an exercise facility. Read as a whole, the most reasonable interpretation of the risk provision was the parties' intention to exculpate the health club from injuries—whether self-inflicted or caused by other members—sustained from the usual activities at a health club. However, the risk section did *not* contemplate releasing the health club from its *own* negligence.

Contractual Ambiguity. The principle of construing contractual ambiguity against the drafting party is well established. When examining a release, it must be clear, explicit, and comprehensible. If an alternative, "semantically reasonable" meaning exists, the release is deemed ambiguous.

In the recreational sports context, parties are free to contractually redistribute risk because release provisions do not implicate the public interest and are therefore not void as against public policy. Provided a release is clear—guaranteeing that both parties contemplated the redistribution of risk—a release can relieve a health club of due care it otherwise would be obligated to provide. However, if a release is ambiguous—and it is not obvious that the parties contemplated redistributing the risk that caused the plaintiff's injury—then the contractual ambiguity should be construed *against* the drafter, rendering the release void.

For example, in a previous case the court found that the collapse of a sauna bench was *not* the type of injury contemplated by a general release provision. The court explained that the health club's "negligence was not reasonably related to the object for which the release was given, that is, injuries resulting from participating in sports or exercise, rather than from merely reclining on the facility's furniture." While it is not necessary that a release articulate every possible act of negligence, the release must clearly contemplate the *type* of injury attributable to a particular act of negligence. When parties intend for such a provision to exceed inherent risks, it is important that those *non-inherent* risks be specified.

Release of Negligence. In the view of the appellate court, the assumption of risk provision did not release LA Workout from its *own* negligence. The provision contemplated injuries to the member caused by others, and injuries to others caused by the member. Zipusch agreed to release LA Workout from the former type of injury and to indemnify LA Workout for the latter. The distinction between the release and the indemnification clauses, the court said, is important. The *release* clause precluded lawsuits against LA Workout from unpreventable injuries caused by third-party conduct in the natural course of exercising. The *indemnification* clause obligated a third party who caused injury to reimburse LA Workout for its share of any judgment.

Zipusch maintained that the exculpatory clause only contemplated injuries arising "from the negligence or other acts of anyone else using LA Workout." This clause, Zipusch argued, did not release LA Workout from its *own* negligence.

In reply, LA Workout reasoned that the release applied because the substance could not have appeared in any other way than third-party conduct. However, the court pointed out that even assuming this was true, the release did not clearly relieve LA Workout from *all* liability caused by a third party, especially in light of the provision which stated that the use of the facility "naturally involves the risk of injury."

In the appellate court's mind, a semantically reasonable interpretation was the parties' intention to release LA Workout from unpreventable injuries caused by *others* in the natural course of exercising. By stating that LA Workout would not be liable for the "natural" risks associated with exercising, the contract merely expressed the obvious. LA Workout had *not* eliminated its duty to *not* enhance the inherent risks of exercising at a health club. In other words, the assumption of risk did *not* explicitly exculpate LA Workout from its *own* negligence.

Disputed Fact Issues

In the end, the appellate court found that Zipusch had raised an issue of material fact, which precluded summary judgment. Circumstantial evidence of a property owner's failure to inspect the premises before an accident is sufficient to infer that the risk existed long enough for the property owner to have discovered and removed it.

In other words, a property owner's failure to reasonably inspect its equipment can constitute *constructive* knowledge of the dangerous condition, providing a causal link between the accident and the time period between inspections. The determination of what constitutes a reasonable time period between inspections will of course vary according to the particular circumstances.

Thus, while a thirty-minute interval between inspections at a busy commercial retail center might lead to an inference of negligence, the same inference might not be found elsewhere. Zipusch had therefore raised an issue of material fact regarding whether LA Workout negligently inspected and maintained its exercise equipment. In the case of a busy health club, a reasonable argument could be made that routine inspection of the premises is important, and that eighty-five minutes is unreasonably long. Likewise, the failure to *ever* inspect the undersides of the treadmill could lead a trier of fact to find that the health club negligently maintained its exercise equipment.

The appellate court thus concluded that the liability release was too ambiguous to insulate the health club from liability for its own negligence and that issues of fact existed about whether the club failed to properly inspect and maintain its equipment. Alas, the resolution of the mysterious substance that supposedly tripped up Yoko Zipusch would have to await another day.

Chapter 2

Release of Liability: Not Your Typical Sports Injury

Benedek v. PLC Santa Monica, 104 Cal. App.4th 1351 (2002)

The well-renowned Pritikin Longevity Center and Spa is decorously located on the grounds of the swanky Santa Monica Beach Hotel. Before his usual workout on the elliptical training machine, a member named Tom Benedek noticed that the large television set overhead was facing the wrong way, so he attempted a slight adjustment, which caused the television to start sliding off its rack. Benedek tried valiantly—but awkwardly—to stop the accelerating force, but he was ultimately unable to bear the weight and injured his knee.

The central issue in the resulting trial was the release of liability. As part of his membership application, Benedek had signed a two-page agreement containing a waiver of liability. In the agreement's initial paragraph, Benedek acknowledged that he was "using the facilities and services of the hotel and the spa at his own risk." The waiver then boldly continued:

> The spa and hotel and their owners, officers, employees, agents, contractors, and affiliates shall not be liable—and

the member hereby expressly waives any claim of liability—
for personal/bodily injury or damages—which occur to any
member, or for any loss of or injury to person or property.
This waiver includes, but is not limited to any loss, damage,
or destruction of the personal property of the member **and
is intended to be a complete release of any responsibil-
ity for personal injuries and/or property loss/damage
sustained by any member while on the hotel and/or spa
premises, whether using exercise equipment or not.**
(emphasis in the original)

Benedek's suit against Pritikin alleged negligence and premises liability. In its answer, the defendant raised the affirmative defenses of
assumption of the risk and release of liability, and then moved for
summary judgment on the grounds that those provisions expressly
negated any duty that Pritikin owed to Benedek.

The trial court granted the defendant's summary judgment
motion, and Benedek appealed.

Liability Releases

The determination of whether a release contains ambiguities is,
the court explained, a simple matter of contractual construction.
If a release concerns *all* liability, then it applies to *any* negligent
act of the defendant. In the trial court's view, the agreement Benedek signed was clear, unambiguous, and explicit, and it released
Pritikin from liability for *any* injuries suffered while on Pritikin's
premises, "whether using exercise equipment or not."

The purpose of the release was to allow Benedek access to
Pritikin's facilities, and there was no question that Benedek was
injured while inside those facilities. On appeal, Benedek contended

that the release should be interpreted to apply *only* to injuries suffered while actively using Pritikin's exercise equipment. The court considered three previous cases:

Leon v. Family Fitness Center (#107), Inc. In this case, the health club member was injured when a sauna bench on which he was laying collapsed. He had signed a release, but the provision was inconspicuously buried in the small print of the agreement. The clause stated: "The member specifically agrees that Family Fitness shall not be liable for any claim, demand, or cause of action for death, personal injury, property damage, or loss of any kind resulting from the member's use of the facilities."

The court concluded that the release was (a) not sufficiently conspicuous to be enforceable, and (b) ambiguous. Noting that the exculpatory clause was sandwiched between two clauses concerning inherent risks in an exercise program—and with no mention that it was intended to insulate the health club from liability for premises negligence—the court held that the release was ineffective to release claims unrelated to exercise activities.

However, the *Leon* court never suggested that a properly drafted release could *not* release a health club from liability for injuries *unrelated* to fitness activities. Indeed, the court strongly suggested otherwise: "Reading the entire document leads to the inescapable conclusion the release does not clearly, explicitly, and comprehensibly set forth that the intent of the document is to release claims for personal injuries resulting from the enterprise's own negligent acts, regardless of whether related to the exercise activities it marketed." The clear implication of *Leon* was that a release clearly setting forth such an intent would be enforceable.

Sanchez v. Bally's Total Fitness Corp. A health club patron had signed a release specifically referring to fitness-related injuries she might suffer. In her lawsuit for injuries sustained during a slide aerobics class, she contended that the release was ineffective because it did not *expressly* refer to the negligence of the health club. The court held that the release was applicable "by its terms and context" to the negligence of the health club. The court stated: "It is obvious that patrons of health clubs sign release provisions in contemplation of injuries that occur in the course of using the facilities for exercising. Therefore, the injury suffered by plaintiff in the present matter is one reasonably within the contemplation of the parties."

Lund v. Bally's Aerobic Plus, Inc. A health club member was injured while using weight-lifting equipment under the allegedly negligent supervision of a personal trainer. The release expressly referred to the "use of any exercise equipment or facilities" and "our negligent instruction or supervision." The plaintiff contended that the contract to obtain the services of the personal trainer was *separate* from the membership agreement; that personal trainer services had not been specifically mentioned in the release; and thus the injuries suffered while being personally trained were *outside* the scope of the release. The court rejected this argument, noting that the incident in which the plaintiff was injured was within the scope of the release and was reasonably related to the purpose for which the release was given.

In the present case, Benedek asserted that health clubs are *prohibited* from contractually reallocating the risks of premises liability. The appellate court strongly disagreed, noting that there is *no* restriction on voluntary agreements in which one party agrees to shoulder a risk that the law would otherwise have placed upon the other party. Therefore, a release of premises liability in consideration for permission to enter the recreational facilities does *not* violate public policy.

The appellate court further reasoned that the plaintiff's argument was not semantically reasonable, and indeed, was contrary to the express language of the release. By its unambiguous and broad language, the release concerned *all* personal injuries on Pritikin's premises—including the injury that Benedek suffered from a falling television. The relevant inquiry, the court said, is *not* whether the injury is reasonably related to the *purpose* of using fitness equipment, but whether it was reasonably related to the *language* of the release. The release signed by Benedek unambiguously released Pritikin from liability for *any* injury Benedek suffered on the premises, whether using exercise equipment or not.

The trial court's judgment was therefore affirmed, and Pritikin was allowed to recover its costs on appeal. The whole incident no doubt created painful memories for Mr. Benedek, who paid dearly for trying to relieve the tedium of exercise by watching a little TV.

Chapter 3

Beware the Window: Working Out in a Crowd

Pappalardo v. New York Health & Racquet Club, 279 A.D.2d 134 (1st Dept. 2000)

Urban health clubs often present a unique set of circumstances for litigators, and the case of Michael Pappalardo is a prime example.

Pappalardo was a long-time member of the very popular New York Health & Racquet Club. One evening, he and a friend, Cheryl Joseph, went there to work out. Just before the accident occurred, Pappalardo was using a "leg curl" machine on the second floor of the gym. The machine was located in a row of approximately ten exercise machines that ran parallel to a large window overlooking East 13th Street. The machine was situated so that the individual using it faced the window, which was only a few feet away. After concluding one set of repetitions, Pappalardo stepped aside so his friend Joseph could begin exercising.

At this point, Pappalardo, in order to find room to stretch his hamstrings, moved toward the window, standing in front of the machine and with his back to the window. Pappalardo then stepped back to tie his shoe, and the glass behind him shattered, causing him to fall to the pavement below. Initially, Pappalardo testified that no part of his body came into contact with the glass, but in a subsequent affidavit, he stated that he "brushed against the window" and "that the window instantly and simultaneously shattered."

Pappalardo sued the health club and its lessor, Fraydun Manocherian, for negligence in failing to: (a) maintain the windows in a safe and proper condition, (b) provide warning devices or barricades in front of the windows, and (c) comply with unspecified statutes and codes.

The defendants thereafter moved for summary judgment on the grounds that (a) there was no evidence that the window was defective, (b) there was no evidence that they had actual or constructive notice of a defect, (c) the plaintiff's fall was not foreseeable, and (d) the health club was not responsible for the maintenance of the windows.

Pappalardo cross-moved for summary judgment on the issue of liability and argued that the window was comprised of improperly thin, non-safety glass, in violation of the administrative code, and that the violation defined the defendants' duty, the breach of that duty, and notice.

The judge granted the defendants' motion and dismissed the complaint, finding: (a) that the defendants had neither actual nor constructive notice of the allegedly dangerous condition, and (b) that the plaintiff failed to establish the applicability of the various provisions of the administrative code.

Administrative Code Violations

Pappalardo provided a laundry list of administrative code sections of which the defendants purportedly ran afoul. Pappalardo further maintained that because of changes made in the certificate of occupancy, the defendants were responsible for bringing the building up to code.

The trial court found, however, that the plaintiff failed to proffer any evidence indicating that the administrative code sections applied to the building in question. (The administrative code had grandfathered in those buildings that existed at the time of the code revision.) Specifically, the court noted that it was unknown what year the building was constructed, or the date and cost of renovations performed by the defendants, all of which were necessary to determine the applicability of the relevant code sections.

On appeal, Pappalardo relied upon the administrative code section which provided: "If the alteration of a building results in a change in the classification of the building, then the *entire* building shall be made to comply with the requirements of the code." (emphasis added)

The appellate court agreed that triable issues of fact existed as to whether the alterations and repairs made to the premises brought it within the purview of the administrative code. Pappalardo had produced evidence indicating that costly alterations made to the premises resulted in a change in the building's classification, as well as evidence indicating that the defendants themselves believed the code applied. As a result, the court concluded that issues of fact existed as to whether the thin windows and lack of safety rails violated the code.

With regard to the owner's claim that he could not be held liable as an out-of-possession landlord who had no notice of the defect, the court noted that "constructive" notice can be found (a) where a specific statutory violation exists, and (b) the out-of-possession landlord reserves a right to enter the premises for inspection and maintenance. For this reason, Pappalardo identified the specific statutory violations (the glass was impermissibly thin, and the windows should have contained a grill or push bars), and the specific lease provisions regarding landlord rights, which stated: "The exterior walls of the building, the portions of any window sills outside the windows, and the windows are not part of the premises demised by this lease and the landlord reserves all rights to such parts of the building." As a result of this evidence, it appeared that the out-of-possession landlord *could* be held liable.

Ultimately, however, the appellate court concluded that Pappalardo had provided *no* proof that the defendants installed the window or had actual knowledge of a defect, and that there was *no* indication that the defect was so apparent it would constitute constructive notice. Absent these statutory violations, Pappalardo's common law negligence claim failed.

As a result, Pappalardo's complaint was reinstated only to the extent that it possibly asserted a negligence claim arising out of statutory violations. The great glass caper, it seemed, would continue on for later resolution. Stay tuned.

Chapter 4

Failure to Spot: A Barbell Tale

Sicard v. University of Dayton, 660 N.E.2d 1241 (Ohio 1995)

It may come as no surprise that lifting extremely heavy weights can be a problem in more ways than one.

Alfred Sicard was a basketball player at the University of Dayton, and in order to keep his scholarship, he was required to work out with weights to stay in shape. On the day in question, Sicard was lying on a bench underneath a 365-pound barbell. As he attempted to press this staggering load, his strength uncharacteristically failed him. Two spotters grabbed the middle and one end of the weight, but they were unable to stop the fall. Dave Bollwinkel, a university employee (and incredibly, his real name), was supposed to assist, but had turned away to talk to someone else.

Sicard suffered a painful ruptured pectoral muscle when this rather weighty force struck his left shoulder. He brought an action against the university and Bollwinkel, alleging that his excruciating injury proximately resulted from Bollwinkel's irresponsible conduct. The defendants moved for summary judgment, and after the trial court granted the motion, Sicard appealed. Sicard argued that Bollwinkel's acts were reckless and wanton, and that such determination involved a genuine issue of material fact to be determined by a jury after presentation of all the evidence.

Weight lifting, the appellate court observed, is not a contact sport, and its participants require spotters to help them initially lift the weight and to avoid injury. Participation in the sport may manifest a willingness to submit to injuries from *lifting* heavy objects, but it does *not* manifest a willingness to submit to injury from *falling* weights. A spotter who intentionally fails to provide the necessary assistance may be liable if he creates an unreasonable risk of harm to the weight lifter.

There was not much dispute about the facts, except whether Bollwinkel agreed to act as a spotter. Sicard and one of the spotters said that he did, but Bollwinkel denied it. Issues of credibility must be resolved against the party who moves for summary judgment, because the non-moving party is entitled to have the evidence construed most strongly in his favor. The court ruled that a reasonable mind could have concluded that Bollwinkel's actions created an unreasonable risk of harm to Sicard because of (a) the weight involved, and (b) Sicard's vulnerability to injury should Bollwinkel fail in his duties.

The court determined that the record ultimately presented genuine issues of material fact, and that the trial court therefore erred when it entered summary judgment for the defendants. As a result, the scrutiny of Mr. Bollwinkel and his allegedly nonobservant ways in the spotting arena would remain for determination by a future tribunal. In the meantime, one wishes Mr. Sicard a speedy recovery so that he can continue pressing weights that are the equivalent of two small refrigerators.

Chapter 5

Premises Liability: The Hazards of Athletic Machines

Forgang v. Universal Gym Co., 621 A.2d 601 (Penn. 1993)

It all began one glorious evening when a college fraternity, known simply by the initials SAR, held a party at the Abbey Racquetball Club in Philadelphia. Prior to the lively event, a rental agreement for the facility was signed by both parties. Because the organization consisted of minors, the contract wisely required the presence of five chaperones at the event. The agreement also explicitly provided that "no physical fitness equipment on the second floor may be used."

During the party, the club was not open to the general public or the club's regular members. Despite the express prohibition against using the fitness equipment, Ilene Forgang decided, for whatever reason, to use the "pec dec" chest press machine. She was promptly struck on both sides of her face by the powerful arms of the machine, which caused serious injuries.

In due course, Forgang filed a complaint against the club, alleging that their negligent conduct was responsible for her problems. At trial, the judge granted the defendant's motion for a directed verdict. The court reasoned that (a) notices were prominently posted on the equipment prohibiting non-members from using the equipment, and (b) Abbey was a landlord out of possession and therefore owed no duty to those on the premises.

On appeal, Forgang argued that disputed issues of fact remained for determination, namely whether the defendant was a landlord out of possession. Forgang asserted that the trial court disregarded evidence indicating that the defendant *retained* control of the premises during the party. Specifically, Forgang pointed to the fact that employees of the club were present during the event, and that there was a provision in the rental agreement in which the club reserved the right to remove anyone who did not comply with the club's rules and regulations.

Interestingly enough, the appellate court agreed with Forgang. The court recounted the rule that generally a landlord out of possession is *not* liable for injuries unless the landlord has retained the right to control the premises. Moreover, a landlord who retains control is only liable if, by the exercise of reasonable care, the landlord could have discovered the risky condition and rendered it safe.

Even though a review of the rental agreement indicated that SAR leased the entire club for the fraternity's party and that the chaperones were responsible for those in attendance, there were several indications that the club had retained control of the premises. An Abbey employee testified that "their job that night was to patrol the place and make sure that things ran right." Employees of Abbey were also told to ask those who did not abide by the rules to leave. One club employee apparently handed out volleyballs and racquetball equipment, while another one walked around the club overseeing the activities. Yet another employee roped off certain equipment during the evening, and one guest even testified that an Abbey employee showed him how to use the banded exercise equipment.

Since there was ample evidence that the club had retained control of the premises, the appellate court reversed and remanded the case for determination of who should be responsible for the injuries caused by the dastardly machine that so violently boxed Ilene Forgang's ears that fateful night in Philadelphia.

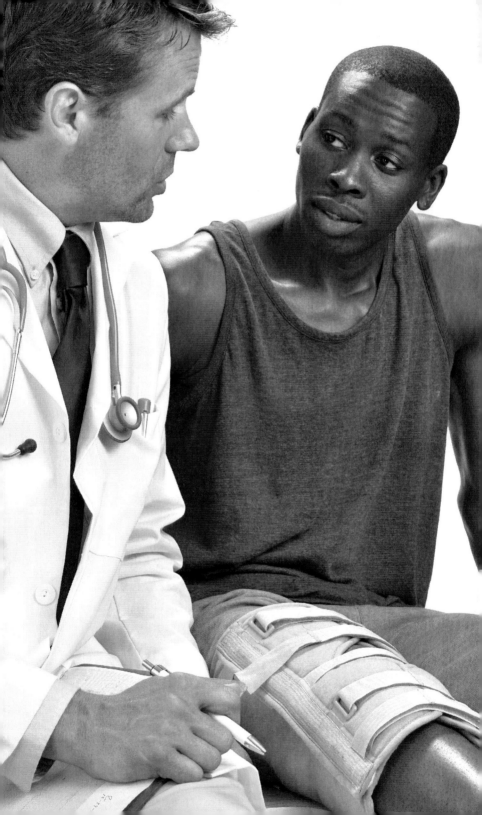

Chapter 6

Medical Emergency: Defining the Duty of Care

L.A. Fitness v. Mayer, 980 So.2d 550 (Fla. 2008)

The L.A. Fitness in Oakland Park, Florida, is typically a placid place, but one spring evening around 9:00 p.m., one of the managers heard someone yell for help. He quickly rose from his desk, calmly instructed the receptionist to call 911, and ran to the back of the gym. There he saw Alessio Tringali, forty-nine years old, lying on his back and surrounded by several members of the gym.

According to the manager, Tringali was bleeding from a cut on his head and shaking from mild convulsions. The manager, who was certified in CPR, believed Tringali was having a seizure or a stroke. He knelt down beside Tringali to assess his condition, and he felt a faint pulse. He also noted the red color of Tringali's face and concluded he was breathing. Because it appeared that Tringali had fallen off a nearby stepping machine and may have suffered a concussion or injured his neck, he did not perform a "chin tilt" to open his airway (one of the first steps in CPR) and possibly make matters worse.

Most witnesses estimated that paramedics arrived within four or five minutes of the call for help. None of the bystanders attempted to get Tringali's vital signs, but simply encouraged him to breathe. When three EMTs arrived, Tringali was not breathing and did not have a pulse. EMS attached an oxygen mask, performed CPR, and employed a defibrillator. Unfortunately, they were unable to reestablish a pulse.

Tringali's daughter, as personal representative of his estate, filed a wrongful death action against L.A. Fitness. She alleged that the company breached its duty to use reasonable care for the safety of the deceased, including the duty to render aid during a medical emergency. Specifically, the plaintiff asserted that L.A. Fitness: (1) failed to properly screen the deceased's health condition at or about the time he joined the health club, (2) failed to administer cardiopulmonary resuscitation, (3) failed to have an automatic external defibrillator (AED) on its premises and to use it on the deceased, and (4) failed to properly train its employees and agents for handling medical emergencies.

Dr. Steven Van Camp, a cardiologist with a special interest in the hazards of exercise, was the plaintiff's medical expert, and he concluded that Tringali—who had no history of heart disease—died as a result of a cardiac arrest, and that the defibrillation later used was not effective because CPR had not been timely and effectively administered. Dr. Van Camp testified that the deceased's cause of death was hypertrophic cardiomyopathy. In Dr. Van Camp's opinion, Tringali's condition was treatable with defibrillation, but if defibrillation was not possible, CPR could have been used to "increase the likelihood that later defibrillation would be successful and to preserve brain function."

Dr. Van Camp explained that "CPR does not correct ventricular fibrillation by itself, but what it does, it prolongs the time for which effective defibrillation can be administered." In Dr. Van Camp's opinion, if CPR alone had been administered before paramedics arrived, there was a 75 percent or greater chance that Tringali would have been successfully resuscitated. Moreover, Tringali likely would have survived for another twenty-five years.

Dr. Max Harry Weil, a cardiologist, agreed that CPR extends the time in which defibrillation can be successfully administered. Dr. Weil testified that "if the defibrillator isn't immediately available, you give yourself a chance to extend the time window over which the defibrillator might be effective. Put another way, that very sharp quoted three-minute interval is then extended to four, five or six minutes." Dr. Weil agreed that Tringali would likely have been revived by paramedics if he had been given CPR by L.A. Fitness employees.

Dr. Anthony Abbott testified that L.A. Fitness was negligent by failing to perform CPR on Tringali. Dr. Abbott, an exercise physiologist and president of Fitness Institute International, testified about the health club industry's standards of care for cardiac safety at such facilities. Dr. Abbott testified that L.A. Fitness violated those standards by failing to have a written emergency plan and to employ qualified personnel for handling emergencies. He said that the standards promulgated by the industry's authorities were directed at responding to cardiopulomonary emergencies because "when people exercise there's a radically increased chance of having a cardiovascular incident because of the increased stress that comes with exercise." Dr. Abbott testified that L.A. Fitness' plan was inadequate.

Dr. Abbott explained the CPR procedure. First, the responder must determine if the individual is responsive. If the individual does not respond, regardless of the reason, the responder must activate the emergency medical service system or call 911. Then, if the individual is not breathing, the responder must administer CPR. Dr. Abbott noted that even though an individual has a heartbeat, his heart will stop if he is not breathing. After the responder determines that CPR is necessary, he must perform a chin lift to open the airway. The responder then puts his ear over the individual's mouth and nose to feel for air, and looks at the individual's chest for movement. Dr. Abbott noted that the L.A. Fitness manager did not perform a chin lift; nor did he assume an appropriate position to note any chest movement. The responder must then ventilate the individual. After ventilating, the responder should determine whether the individual's heart is beating by looking for movement of the body and checking for a pulse at the carotid artery in the neck. Abbot testified that, in addition to failing to have a written emergency plan or qualified responders, L.A. Fitness fell below the industry's standards of care by failing to have an automated external defibrillator on its premises. Dr. Abbott admitted that such devices were not then required by law, and that L.A. Fitness employees were not required by law to perform CPR or to have a written emergency plan.

Abbot further testified that L.A. Fitness fell below the pertinent standards by failing to screen individuals prior to their commencing exercise and by failing to employ a medical liaison. Dr. Abbott admitted on cross-examination that he could not quantify the number of similar facilities that screened members. He also admitted that none of the deceased's doctors had detected his heart condition.

Dr. Nicholas Fortuin, a cardiovascular disease and internal medicine specialist, testified for the defense. He said that individuals with undiagnosed hypertrophic cardiomyopathy are at greater risk of ventricular fibrillation during strenuous exercise than are other individuals. He further stated that the chances of recovery from cardiac arrest due to hypertrophic cardiomyopathy are much less than arrest caused by other heart diseases. He estimated Tringali's survival at less than 10 percent. Dr. Fortuin further explained that in Tringali's case, even if an AED had been used, more likely than not, he would not have been resuscitated because of the type and severity of his heart disease.

After both sides rested, the jury returned a verdict finding that Tringali's death was caused by the negligence of L.A. Fitness (85 percent) as well as the deceased (15 percent). The jury awarded Tringali's daughter Lenora $100,000 for lost support and services in the past, and $300,000 for future support and services. The jury further awarded Tringali's wife $100,000 for pain and suffering in the past and $200,000 for future pain and suffering. Alessio Tringali, the son, was awarded $25,000 for past pain and suffering. Total damages awarded were $729,000. Following the verdict, the court denied L.A. Fitness' motion for entry of judgment, or for a new trial, or remittitur. The court entered a final judgment for the plaintiff for $619,650.

L.A. Fitness appealed from the judgment, contending that it satisfied its duty to render assistance to the deceased as a matter of law when it promptly summoned professional medical assistance for him. The plaintiff cross-appealed, contending that the trial court erroneously instructed the jury on comparative negligence.

The appeal raised a question concerning the duty a health club or gym owes to a patron who is injured while exercising on its premises. L.A. Fitness argued that the trial court erred in not directing a verdict as a matter of law in its favor because it did not breach its duty of reasonable care to Tringali. Both parties recognized that a "special relationship" existed between L.A. Fitness and its members, and that, as with any business owner, L.A. Fitness had a duty to use reasonable care in rendering aid to Tringali when he became ill or injured. The parties disagreed, however, as to the nature and extent of the duty owed the deceased and whether L.A. Fitness breached that duty.

The CPR Issue

The issue of the duty owed by a health club owner to an injured patron was a case of first impression for the court, and neither party provided any statutory or case law in Florida that clearly delineated the duties owed by a health club or gym to patrons facing a medical emergency. L.A. Fitness employees immediately advised their staff to call 911 when they heard a call for help and then quickly ran over to Tringali to check his condition. One employee felt Tringali's wrist, noted his breathing patterns and heartbeat, saw the head cut, noted his position on his back, observed his facial color, and decided not to attempt CPR, as he believed it was unnecessary and could worsen his condition. He stayed with Tringali and continued to monitor his condition until the paramedics arrived within a few minutes after they were called. This undisputed evidence, according to L.A. Fitness, showed that it fulfilled its common law duty to render aid and secure medical assistance for Tringali.

The court found no precedent for imposing the duty the plaintiff proposed in this case. None of the authorities cited by the plaintiff supported imposing a duty upon health clubs to have CPR-trained employees on site for medical emergencies and to require employees (who generally lack medical training) to perform CPR on injured patrons. At trial, the plaintiff presented expert testimony about health club industry standards and recommendations regarding CPR.

Although the custom and practice of an industry can help define a standard of care a party must exercise after it has undertaken a duty, industry standards do not give rise to an independent legal duty. Courts in other jurisdictions have generally held that a business owner satisfies its legal duty to come to the aid of a patron experiencing a medical emergency by summoning medical assistance within a reasonable time. They have declined to extend the duty of reasonable care to include providing medical care.

The court remarked that even if it construed the Restatement's obligation to provide "first aid" to business invitees, they would nonetheless conclude that such obligation does not encompass the duty to perform skilled treatment, such as CPR, which requires training, because it is more than mere "first aid." Although the procedure for CPR is relatively simple and widely known as a major technique for saving lives, it nonetheless requires training and re-certification. Unlike first responders, for whom performing CPR is routine, non-medical employees certified in CPR remain laymen and should retain their discretion in deciding when to utilize the procedure.

Negligent Undertaking

The plaintiff then argued that even if L.A. Fitness's common law duty of care to Tringali did not require it to administer CPR, L.A. Fitness voluntarily assumed a duty to perform CPR. The plaintiff contended that once the health club employee undertook to assist Tringali, he had a duty to perform CPR with reasonable care. Florida law required that an action undertaken for the benefit of another, even gratuitously, be performed in accordance with an obligation to exercise reasonable care.

L.A. Fitness argued that its employees' actions in checking on Tringali did not amount to an undertaking to perform CPR on him. The L.A. Fitness manager took the preliminary step of assessing the situation of the decedent, including taking his pulse. The question was whether that assessment committed him to performing CPR if that was indicated. The court did not believe that it did. The plaintiff did not establish that the health club worsened Tringali's condition or caused others to refrain from rendering aid.

Defibrillators

The plaintiff also asserted that L.A. Fitness's duty of reasonable care required it to have an automatic external defibrillator (AED) on its premises and to use it on the deceased. The court pointed out that there was no common law or statutory duty that a business have such a device on its premises. To the contrary, the Florida legislature had adopted the "Cardiac Arrest Survival Act," which did not require that an AED be placed in any building or location or that an acquirer of an AED have persons trained in its use.

In sum, the court concluded that, under the circumstances presented, L.A. Fitness fulfilled its duty of reasonable care in rendering aid to the deceased by summoning paramedics within a reasonable time. L.A. Fitness did not have a legal duty to have CPR-qualified employees on site at all times, and their employees were under no legal duty to administer CPR to the deceased. Furthermore, L.A. Fitness had no legal duty to have a defibrillator on the premises for emergency use on the deceased. The case was accordingly reversed.

Part II

Running

Chapter 7

Fore!: Runners and Flying Golf Balls

McGuire v. New Orleans City Park Improvement Assn., 835 So.2d 416 (La. 2003)

Being hit by an errant golf ball is rarely a concern for runners, but there is always an exception to every rule.

One fine spring morning in Louisiana, Robert McGuire was jogging on Palm Drive in New Orleans City Park near the Bayou Oaks Golf Course. As he did most mornings, McGuire crossed the bridge near South Course Hole No. 3. But the run was a little different this time—a golf ball landed on the roadway in front of him, bounced, and then hit him in the groin area (ouch!), an undoubtedly painful injury that required surgery.

McGuire filed suit against the New Orleans City Park Improvement Association, the operators of the golf course, and its insurer for damages, alleging that the Park association breached its duties to (1) warn non-golfers of the danger of flying golf balls, (2) configure the golf course such that a danger was not created for non-golfers, and (3) provide a protective barrier between the golf course and Palm Drive.

In its defense, City Park maintained that: (1) McGuire jogged through the golf course between two clearly visible greens, which were not a hidden peril that required a warning or protective barrier, (2) the risk was an ordinary one, and (3) it was not reasonably foreseeable that a golfer would hit a ball so far to the right that a non-golfer would be struck.

This issue was a new one for the court. In other jurisdictions, golf course owners had occasionally been found liable to non-golfers for failing to maintain the premises in a reasonably safe condition. In one case, the owners were held liable when a car passenger was struck in the eye by a golf ball while the vehicle was in a clubhouse driveway near a fairway. The court noted that there were no warnings to motorists and no special rule of play at the hole. In another case, a golf course owner was liable to an automobile passenger who was struck by a ball near a hole that was adjacent to a busy highway. And in yet another case, a golf course owner was held liable when a boater, traveling down a river that flowed through a golf course, was struck by a golf ball, and no warning signs were posted.

After a trial on the merits, the jury found City Park negligent and awarded McGuire the sum of $75,000, which included the following damages: $13,750 for past, present, and future physical pain and suffering; $15,000 for past, present, and future mental distress; $30,000 for past medical expenses; and $16,250 for permanent disfigurement. The jury determined that City Park was 40 percent at fault and McGuire 60 percent. City Park filed a motion for judgment notwithstanding the verdict. A remittitur was granted, which reduced the medical expenses from $30,000 to $11,680. City Park appealed the ruling.

The intermediate appellate court held that City Park owed a duty to a "passer-by not playing golf and not on the golf course" to exercise reasonable and ordinary care to keep the premises reasonably safe and take reasonable precautions. The court found no manifest error in the jury's allocation of fault. Dissatisfied with the ruling, the defendant then appealed the case to the Louisiana Supreme Court.

Duty-Risk Analysis

The Supreme Court began its duty-risk analysis by examining the duty owed by City Park to the non-golfer. City Park argued that it had no duty to protect a non-golfer against injury from an errant golf shot because the risk was "obvious, reasonable, and minuscule." City Park agreed that it had a duty to discover, correct, and warn of any *unreasonably* dangerous condition, but contended that it acted with reasonable care under the circumstances. In the alternative, City Park argued that if it had a duty to warn of hidden dangers, it fulfilled that duty by adequately warning entrants when it (a) erected signs ("golfers only beyond this point" and "golf cart crossings"), and (b) designed the golf course so as to avoid the possibility of injury.

The court ultimately reached the conclusion that McGuire was precluded from recovery because of his familiarity with the park and the golf course. McGuire admitted that he grew up near City Park, lived thirteen years of his adult life a mile away, had frequently jogged that same route, knew that it traversed a golf course, and observed golfers as he was jogging that day. The court concluded that McGuire was adequately warned and should have anticipated golf balls when jogging near the vicinity of a golf course. Under these circumstances, City Park owed *no* duty to provide additional warnings.

The court pointed out that the proposed remedies—erecting barriers, reconfiguring the golf course, or closing off the street to pedestrians and bicyclists—were unreasonable because: (1) barriers would be required on both sides of the road to effectively protect non-golfers from an accidental injury, (2) high barriers would substantially interfere with the game of golf, and (3) the cost of the barriers would be prohibitive, considering there had been no such reported accidents in the history of City Park.

With regard to reconfiguring the park, several individuals testified that the four golf courses have had the same layout for over seventy-five years. The designs had never been substantially altered because of any unreasonable danger to a non-golfer, and the safety measures were no different than any other public golf course. The park attracted approximately fourteen million visitors a year with no pedestrian injuries reported.

The court also noted that the park's purpose was to provide the maximum number of recreational opportunities for the greatest number of people. City Park was an unfunded state agency, and golf was the largest single source of revenue. If the roads were closed to pedestrians, barricades erected, or the golf courses redesigned, golfing would end, and the park would have to close.

For these reasons, the Louisiana Supreme Court found that City Park did not breach a duty to Mr. McGuire, who might be well advised that when jogging near golf courses in the future, he should wear clothing that is heavily padded.

Chapter 8

Into a Hole: The Perils of Jogging

Fritscher v. Chateau Golf/Country Club, 453
So. 2d 964 (La. 1984)

On January 28, 1981, Michael Fritscher sustained serious injuries
from an unusual accident—he fell into an open drain hole while
jogging at night on a golf course near his home in Louisiana.

Unfortunately, Fritscher's injuries were quite severe, and an
orthopedic surgeon who examined him immediately after the accident sent him to the emergency room. Their report indicated that
Fritscher had spasms in the paravertebral muscles of his neck and
numbness around his lips. When his condition did not improve, he
saw a neurosurgeon, Dr. Carlos Pisarello. Fritscher complained of
pain in the neck, numbness of all fingers, tingling in his feet, and
a constant headache. Dr. Pisarello determined that the injuries
were the result of a "central cord syndrome."

Following a period of extended treatment, the plaintiff filed
suit against Chateau Golf & Country Club and U.S. Fire Insurance Company. After a trial on the merits, the jury found in favor
of Fritscher. The jury awarded him $400,000 for general damages
and $430,000 for special damages. U.S. Fire placed its policy limits
in the registry of the court, and Chateau appealed the judgment.

Two major issues were presented on appeal: (1) whether the trial judge erred in refusing to present the jury with the defense of assumption of risk, and (2) whether the jury abused its discretion in finding the plaintiff 5 percent negligent.

Assumption of Risk

During cross-examination, Fritscher admitted he knew of the drain hole and the fact that the drain cover was *not* on it. He testified he first noticed the hole without a cover the previous spring. That summer, he complained to the club about it. Ironically, he and one of his neighbors even warned the club that someone could kill himself falling into the hole.

The record further reflected that there was tall grass surrounding the drain hole, but immediately prior to the accident, the grass was cut. Fritscher's testing was pertinent in this regard:

Q. Now, was there anything different about the hole on the night of the accident?

A. Well, it changed considerably.

Q. What happened?

A. Well, I had noticed it that night. What I'm trying to say is it was all manicured, cut.

Q. It's all right to tell me what you might do, but don't have to give the . . .

A. Well, you know, I don't never—you know, the tall grass was a warning to me that there possibly could be a danger there and that morning it was gone, that night when I was jogging.

Q. All right.

A. You know, I hadn't recognized the—I hadn't had the hole on my mind when I completed my exercise that night.

After careful review of all the evidence, the court concluded that Fritscher did *not* assume the risk. While aware of the hole's existence, Fritscher normally identified the hole's location by the tall grass surrounding it. The record reflected that the tall grass was cut immediately prior to Fritscher's accident. The testimony indicated that Fritscher may have known that the tall grass was cut prior to his run, but there was not sufficient evidence to indicate that he truly appreciated and assumed the risk of that danger.

Comparative Negligence

The jury therefore found that Fritscher was only 5 percent negligent. The country club claimed that the jury erred in failing to find that Fritscher's damages were substantially caused by his own negligence, which the club believed to be at least 50 percent of his damages. The defendant also argued that Fritscher had not acted reasonably, since he was aware of the open drain hole, lived only a few feet from the hole, and yet still jogged in the area.

Considering all the parameters of this case—especially the fact that Fritscher was accustomed to the tall grass near the hole—the court refused to declare that the jury erred in finding Fritscher only 5 percent negligent. The judgment in favor of the unfortunate Mr. Fritscher was accordingly affirmed, and the country club no doubt would listen more carefully to future complaints about large holes in the ground.

Chapter 9

Failure to Warn: Using the Mini-Trampoline

Richter v. Limax International, Inc., 45 F.3d 1464 (10th Cir. 1995)

A plaintiff named Dearmedia Richter (you can't make up this sort of thing) claimed that repetitive use of a miniature trampoline caused stress fractures in her ankles. So she promptly sued the manufacturer, Limax International, alleging that the product was defectively designed and contained an inadequate warning.

It was revealed at trial that there were no instructions in the box that contained the trampoline, although affixed to the product itself was a sticker stating that it was designed to be used only as an exercise device. Richter only used the trampoline for jogging, and eventually she increased her time up to an hour a day. She then experienced severe pain in her ankles, and a doctor diagnosed her malady as stress fractures.

Richter produced expert testimony that showed that a jogger's foot striking the trampoline's surface caused the inside of the foot to drop further than the outside. This rotation, called "eversion," occurs to some degree in normal running, but rebound jogging markedly accentuates it. Lateral pulling on an ankle bone by lig aments or muscles can cause microscopic fractures, and if the bone is not allowed to heal, these tiny fractures can coalesce into a stress fracture. Richter's expert witnesses testified that long-term use of the trampoline could affect the ankle bones, and this testimony—interpreted in light of well-established knowledge about the structure of the foot—made it apparent that repetitive use of a mini-trampoline *could* cause stress fractures. Limax admitted that it conducted no tests relating to the long-term effects of jogging on the trampoline and that it did not systematically monitor such studies.

The CEO of Limax testified that the company had sold approximately two million units world-wide and that Richter's complaint about stress fractures was the first it had received. Further, although mini-trampolines had been in use since 1975, no one had suggested a risk of fractures. No expert testifying at trial could identify any study on rebound jogging that suggested such injury.

The case went to trial, and the jury found that the mini-trampoline was not defectively designed, but that Limax was liable under theories of strict liability and negligence for its failure to warn. The jury determined that Richter's damages were $472,712, which was reduced by her contributory negligence of 38 percent.

Limax moved for judgment as a matter of law, which the district court granted. The court concluded the defendant had *no* duty to warn because the plaintiff failed to prove (a) that Limax had knowledge of the danger, or (b) that the danger was known in the state of the art. The court further concluded that Kansas law did not impose a duty on manufacturers to warn about dangers they might have discovered by conducting tests.

The Duty to Test

Richter appealed, contending that Kansas law imposed a duty on manufacturers to test their products and warn consumers accordingly. Richter referred the court to the case of *Wooderson v. Ortho Pharmaceutical Corp.*, where the Kansas Supreme Court held that a drug company had a duty to warn the medical profession about what "it knows, has reason to know, or should know, based upon its position as an expert in the field, upon its research, upon cases reported to it, and upon scientific development, research, and publications in the field." Richter interpreted the language "upon its research" to require manufacturers to test their products for the potential to injure consumers.

The district court in the present case held that Kansas law does *not* require a manufacturer to test its products for dangers not otherwise known in the "state of the art." The court concluded that, because no one was aware of the possibility that jogging on a minitrampoline could cause stress fractures, there was no duty to warn.

The Tenth Circuit saw the situation a little differently. It held that a manufacturer *does* have a duty under Kansas law to warn consumers when it knows (or has reason to know) that its product is dangerous during normal use. This duty to warn is a continuous one, requiring the manufacturer to keep abreast of the current state of knowledge about its products, as acquired through research, adverse reaction reports, scientific literature, and so forth. A manufacturer's failure to adequately warn of its product's reasonably foreseeable dangers renders that product defective under the doctrine of strict liability.

The court noted that the mini-trampoline at issue was specifically intended for exercise, and in particular, for jogging. When used for this purpose, however, the product's design resulted in the foot turning in a way that placed stress on the ankle bones. The fact that the design was not defective (at least within the state of the known art) did *not* detract from the manufacturer's duty to warn the consumer of foreseeable dangers that *could* arise from normal use.

Sufficiency of the Evidence

Given that repetitive jogging on a miniature trampoline could cause stress fractures, the question became whether Richter presented sufficient evidence that a jury could conclude that reasonable tests would have been effective in bringing this danger to light. Richter presented a substantial amount of expert testimony to the effect that visual observation by someone with an expertise in biomechanics would reveal eversion.

The testimony at trial established that it was well-known that such repetitive stresses could cause fractures. A simple consultation with a biomechanics expert would have given Limax sufficient information to arrange for appropriate testing of the device. While it was true that no one considered the problem until Richter's injury occurred, it was also true that the plaintiff's evidence demonstrated that the danger was patently obvious to any expert who looked at it.

The Tenth Circuit concluded that there existed substantial evidence from which the jury could find that the harm was foreseeable. Accordingly, the judgment would be reinstated in favor of Ms. Richter, ankle-challenged as she now sadly was.

Chapter 10

Clothing-Optional Running: Or Not

McGuire v. State, 489 So.2d 729 (Fla. 1986)

For as long as anyone could remember, the northern half of Florida's Air Force Beach was "clothing optional." But when the beach was incorporated into a state recreation area, the dress code changed dramatically. One of the first victims of this stricter regime was Belinda McGuire—she was issued a ticket for jogging without a top.

McGuire was cited for violating rule 16D-2.04(1)(e) of the Florida Administrative Code, which stated: "In every bathing area all persons shall be clothed as to prevent any indecent exposure of the person. All bathing costumes shall conform to commonly accepted standards at all times." (You know an ordinance has been around a while when it uses the term "bathing costumes.")

At trial, McGuire challenged the rule as unconstitutional on the grounds of vagueness. She contended the provision was overbroad because it could be extended beyond nude sunbathing to the wearing of "provocative" swim attire. McGuire conceded that nudity is not in and of itself a constitutionally protected activity and that topless jogging could be legitimately prohibited by a well-drawn rule. But she wished to step into the shoes of other beach-goers who might inadvertently violate the ordinance by wearing "unduly provocative bathing attire."

Nudity, the court agreed, is protected as speech only when combined with some form of expression. Accordingly, the courts have uniformly held that unassociated nudity is subject to government limitations. In light of this lack of constitutional protection, McGuire had to demonstrate that the statute was unconstitutionally vague as it applied to her.

Generally speaking, a vagueness inquiry focuses on situations where one cannot reasonably understand the conduct that is proscribed. McGuire argued that the phrase "shall conform to commonly accepted standards at all times" is so vague that she did not know that topless jogging and sunbathing on a public beach were prohibited. The court found this argument somewhat incredulous in light of the fact that two weeks earlier, McGuire received a warning from the park manager for sunbathing topless at Air Force Beach. Besides, the court said, any person of common intelligence would know from the posted notices that a female is prohibited from jogging topless on the beach.

The court concluded that the state could have used more precise language in drafting the rule. However, the regulation of public nudity, the court said, remains within the ambit of the government's police power, and the court would not second-guess the specific language used by the legislature in regulating such activity.

Ultimately, the court concluded that McGuire had failed to demonstrate that the regulation was so vague that it failed to put her on notice that her activities were proscribed. The court seemed especially miffed by the fact that this peripatetic nudist had been cited for her infraction just a few days earlier, albeit in a more sedentary position.

Chapter 11

A Little Obsessive: The Need to Run

Fisher v. Parks, 618 N.E.2d 1202 (Ill. 1993)

Dr. Jeffrey Fisher loved to run—so much, in fact, that he lost his job as a result of it. Dr. Fisher was forced to file suit against his pathologist partners, Dr. Harry Parks and Dr. Steven Nuernberger, alleging that they wrongfully expelled him from the partnership and failed to account for his financial interest in the business.

The trial court entered judgment for the defendants, and Dr. Fisher appealed

The first issue on appeal was whether the trial court erred in finding that the defendants complied with the terms of the partnership agreement. Specifically, Dr. Fisher argued that the notices of expulsion were not in accordance with the agreement and that he was wrongfully denied a sixty-day probationary period. The appellate court turned to the testimony introduced at trial.

It appeared that the three pathologists entered into a partnership agreement to provide clinical pathology services under the name of Southern Illinois Medical Business Associates (SIMBA). At each hospital that SIMBA serviced, pathologists operated the hospital's laboratory, supervised and trained hospital lab personnel, participated in the training of medical staff, and undertook any clinical pathology while on duty. They were also on call to perform autopsies. The duties of the three partners were rotated. Neither Dr. Parks nor Dr. Nuernberger had any criticism of Dr. Fisher's performance during his first year with the partnership.

But then things changed. There arose a number of complaints about Dr. Fisher in regard to his dereliction of duties, at the laboratory or in servicing client hospitals, in order that Dr. Fisher could go jogging. For example:

- Sparta Community Hospital complained that Dr. Fisher failed to attend certain meetings, and it appeared that SIMBA could forfeit its contract with the hospital if these actions continued.
- Mary Cruzvergara, Ruth Joachimsthaler, and Arna Trotter, employees of SIMBA, testified that, because of Dr. Fisher's jogging activities, there were times when he could not be reached. They testified that, although the laboratory hours were from 8 a.m. to 5 p.m., Dr. Fisher usually spent only six hours at the laboratory, which included the forty-five minutes to an hour and a half that he spent jogging.
- There was testimony that Dr. Fisher jogged while he was on duty at client hospitals. A medical technologist at St. Joseph's Hospital said that Dr. Fisher went out jogging more than half the times he visited the hospital and would do so shortly after he arrived. On a number of occasions she had to tell physicians that Dr. Fisher was unavailable because he was out jogging. Another medical technologist testified that Dr. Fisher went jogging nearly every time he visited the hospital. Due to his jogging, he was unavailable for meetings with the staff.
- The chief executive officer of one hospital testified that, during the time SIMBA provided services to the hospital, he was

critical of only one pathologist—Dr. Fisher. He testified that Dr. Fisher would spend minimal time at the hospital and was not fulfilling SIMBA's contractual obligations. This caused the hospital to rewrite the contract with SIMBA to specify more clearly the length of time a physician was required to spend at the hospital.

- A crime-scene technician for the state of Illinois testified Dr. Fisher did not wait for the technician to present evidence of the crime-scene investigation, but rendered his report without that information. As a result, Dr. Fisher's autopsy report was erroneous because he showed the entry and exit wounds in reverse.

- An assistant coroner testified that Dr. Fisher was always in a hurry and that he always talked of jogging. The coroner recounted an occasion where he needed to have a body re-x-rayed, but that Dr. Fisher did not want to wait the half hour. As a result, he preferred that Dr. Fisher not perform autopsies.

- SIMBA received a letter from the director of laboratories at a hospital describing an incident in which Dr. Fisher failed to send tissue from a malignant adenocarcinoma to clinical laboratories in St. Louis for estrogen and progesterone receptor assays. Dr. Fisher also gave the impression that he was terribly rushed and really did not have time to deal with the load of work confronting him.

As a result of Dr. Fisher's continued disinterest in doing his job because of his jogging diversions, Dr. Nuernberger and Dr. Parks decided to expel Dr. Fisher from the partnership. The two testified that they held an informal meeting on November 5, 1980, to discuss Dr. Fisher's deficiencies. Dr. Fisher was not advised of the meeting.

As a result of their meeting, Dr. Nuernberger and Parks sent Dr. Fisher a letter by certified mail, dated November 5, 1980, which provided as follows:

> This is to give Dr. Fisher a 60-day written notice of expulsion according to the contract signed by Dr. Fisher, Dr. Nuernberger, and Dr. Parks.

It is felt by the remaining partners that Dr. Fisher has continuously failed to fulfill his obligations and duties as a partner. He has purposely and repeatedly failed to cover SIMBA Laboratory when assigned on the schedule, he has caused SIMBA to be fined by an administrator, thus tarnishing the excellent reputation SIMBA enjoys, he has refused to perform autopsies in a prompt and timely manner, thus straining SIMBA's relationship to the various coroners served, and he has repeatedly set a bad example for SIMBA employees by his repeated tardiness to work and early exits from the laboratory. Thus, his overall attitude is incompatible with the values vital to the well-being of SIMBA Laboratory and this partnership.

We, the remaining partners, therefore, are giving Dr. Fisher the sixty-day (60) written notice of expulsion required by our contract with him.

On November 7, 1980, the three partners met to discuss the notice of expulsion. Notes of the meeting revealed that Dr. Fisher denied most of the allegations against him. Dr. Nuernberger and Parks testified that Dr. Fisher's conduct did not change during the ensuing months. For example, on Sunday, November 16, 1980, Dr. Fisher was on call to perform two autopsies the next day, but could not be located. On November 18, 1980, a tissue sample under Dr. Fisher's care was lost.

On January 6, 1981, Dr. Parks and Dr. Nuernberger hand-delivered a letter to Dr. Fisher which provided: "In accordance with our partnership agreement, following a 60-day probation period after written notice of expulsion, we are giving our notice in writing of our final decision in regard to the previous notice of expulsion and will expect that your partnership will terminate Friday, March 6, 1981."

Dr. Fisher argued on appeal that Dr. Parks and Dr. Nuernberger did not comply with the procedural requirements for partner expulsion. The appellate court pointed out that a partnership is controlled by the terms of the agreement under which it is formed and that, because a partnership is a contractual relationship, the principles of contract law fully apply to it.

According to the partnership agreement, the other partners had to first provide Dr. Fisher with written notice of Dr. Fisher's failure to fulfill obligations. The court agreed that the November 5, 1980, letter fulfilled the notice provision. The initial notice was a threshold requirement for commencing the expulsion procedures. It commenced a 60-day period wherein the partner could attempt to cure his deficiencies. The second notice, which was also required to be in writing, was to advise the subject partner what the grounds for expulsion were, and this expulsion notice had to be given 60 days prior to the date of expulsion. Expulsion could only be by majority vote after a finding that the occurrence of the event listed in the initial notice had occurred.

Dr. Fisher contended that the November 5, 1980, notice of expulsion was not issued in compliance with the partnership agreement because it was never discussed at a meeting of all the partners, it was never the subject of a partnership vote, and it did not provide for a 60-day probationary period. As to the charge that the expulsion notice was never discussed prior to issuance, Dr. Fisher argued that Dr. Parks and Dr. Nuernberger met secretly on November 5 and unlawfully deprived Dr. Fisher of his right to respond to allegations of his deficient performance.

Dr. Nuernberger and Dr. Parks argued that there was no provision in the contract for a meeting to discuss the preparation of written notice of partnership failure or for the issuance of a notice of expulsion. The appellate court agreed. The court remarked that the partnership agreement provided that special meetings may be called by any partner. The partnership agreement did not specify that a special meeting had to be called to discuss the preparation of a notice of a partner's deficiencies or of an initial notice of expulsion.

Although a vote of all partners was not required, Dr. Nuernberger and Dr. Parks testified that they voted to send Dr. Fisher the notice. As for the plaintiff's contention that the notice did not advise him of a 60-day probationary period, the court looked to the plain and ordinary meaning of the contract. The partnership agreement specified that a partner could be expelled when his failure to fulfill obligations is "continued for a period of 60 days after written notice thereof." The agreement did not mandate that the notice advise him of a 60-day probationary period.

Dr. Fisher did not dispute that he was familiar with the partnership agreement and that he received the November 5, 1980, letter advising him of alleged deficiencies in his performance. The appellate court found that the trial court did not err in finding that the November 5 letter was satisfactory notice under the contract.

Dr. Fisher also alleged that the letter of January 6, 1981, was not in compliance with the partnership agreement. He argued that he received no notice of a meeting to discuss issuance of the January 6 letter, that there was no notice of a vote, and that, in fact, no partnership vote was taken. It was undisputed that the January 6, 1981, letter required the defaulting partner to be expelled by a majority of the partners, with each partner having one vote. The notice of expulsion had to be delivered, in writing, by registered or certified mail; set forth the grounds for expulsion; and give the subject partner 60-days' notice of the date of expulsion. The contract's expulsion provision did *not* require that a meeting be held or even that a formal partnership vote be taken. A vote of the majority of the partnership members was required to expel. In the view of the appellate court, the evidence demonstrated that Dr. Parks and Dr. Nuernberger voted to expel Dr. Fisher—thus, the voting requirement was satisfied.

The plaintiff's final attack on the January 6 notice was that it failed to set forth the grounds for expulsion. The January 6 letter provided in part: "We are giving our notice in writing of our final decision in regard to previous notice of expulsion." Although the notice did not expressly enumerate the grounds as set forth in the November 5 notice, the November 5 notice was specifically referred to and incorporated therein. The appellate court found that just as a contract may incorporate another document by reference, the January 6 letter incorporated the letter of November 5 by reference. The court concluded that the trial court's determination that the letter of January 6 was sufficient notice under the partnership agreement was not against the manifest weight of the evidence.

The second issue on appeal was whether the trial court erred in finding that Dr. Fisher failed to meet his obligations under the partnership agreement. Dr. Fisher argued that he did not neglect any management obligations during the probationary period from November 5, 1980, through January 6, 1981. Dr. Fisher conceded there were only two purported failures that could remotely be identified as having occurred during the probationary period: the lost-specimen incident, and the failure to perform a Sunday autopsy.

Dr. Fisher contended that these two incidents were inapplicable to establishing his failure to meet management obligations cited in the November 5, 1980, notice. On the contrary, the court said, it was evident that the two alleged incidents occurred during the probationary period and were directly related to Dr. Fisher's failure to fulfill his obligations and duties as a partner under the terms of the partnership agreement. In addition, the notice of November 5 specifically referred to Dr. Fisher's failure to perform autopsies in a prompt and timely manner and his failure to fulfill his obligations and duties as a partner in general. Once again, the appellate court turned to the testimony rendered at trial. Dr. Nuernberger and Dr. Parks testified that after November 5, 1980, Dr. Fisher did not give them any reason to believe he intended to change his unsatisfactory behavior.

Based on the record, the appellate court concluded that the trial court's determination that Dr. Fisher failed his management obligations was not against the manifest weight of the evidence. The judgment of the circuit court was affirmed, and presumably, Dr. Fisher did what he normally did—he went for a run.

Part III

Sports World

Chapter 12

Tennis Ball Retrieval: A Question of Causation

Hueston v. Narragansett Tennis Club, 502 A.2d 827 (R.I. 1986)

The sport of tennis (with the exception of routine elbow and knee problems) is a fairly safe endeavor, but Carol Hueston, an avid player and an active member of Rhode Island's Narragansett Tennis Club, might beg to differ.

Hueston suffered a severe avulsion of the little finger on her left hand while retrieving a tennis ball. She sued the club and claimed that she had sustained severe and permanent bodily injury, disfigurement, severe pain and suffering, and mental anguish and embarrassment—not to mention lost wages and medical expenses.

The case came down to an issue of building construction. Horizontal and vertical girders supported the walls of the building, and several witnesses testified that balls would, on occasion, lodge in the channel formed by the uppermost horizontal girder. The structure and position of the horizontal girders were of particular importance to the case. John Alfano, a registered professional engineer, testified that the second horizontal girder was approximately seven feet above floor level. Each girder was U-shaped, forming a channel seven inches wide and two and a half inches deep. A metal lip at the edge of the channel opening protruded inward three-quarters of an inch.

Hueston testified that on the date of her injury, she went to retrieve a ball that had lodged in the girder. She explained that she had done this in the past, and that she had observed many others (including teaching professionals) do the same. Her injury occurred after her teammate boosted her up so she could stand on the first girder. Hueston then reached up into the girder channel, retrieved the ball, and tossed it to her teammate. She then, while still facing the girder, let go with her right hand and jumped back. As she jumped, the ring on her left little finger caught on the girder lip, and the injury occurred.

Dr. Vincent Iacono, the plaintiff's physician, testified that Hueston provided him with a slightly different version of the event. According to him, Hueston stated that she was injured when she lost her balance, slipped, and grasped for the girder. The tennis club's president maintained that the club had a policy of replacing trapped balls, if requested. Several club members testified that they knew of no such policy, and the club vice-president confirmed that no warning notice had ever been posted to prohibit climbing onto the lower girder or to state that it was dangerous to do so. Alfano, the engineer, testified that blocks of wood could have been placed in the girder channel to prevent balls from accumulating there at a cost of about $180 per court.

The jury answered special interrogatories, finding the plaintiff 25 percent negligent and the defendant 75 percent negligent, and assessed damages at $100,000. Judgment for Hueston was therefore entered in the sum of $75,000.

The defendant contended that the trial judge erred in instructing the jury on the law. Specifically, the defendant argued that the judge incorrectly instructed the jury regarding the doctrines of standard of care, foreseeability, proximate cause, and remote or intervening causes. The defendant also asserted that, since the plaintiff assumed the risk, the trial justice improperly denied its motion for a directed verdict.

The defendant argued that the plaintiff's actions must be measured by the "prudent person rule," and that the trial justice's references to a "reasonable, prudent tennis player" established a specialized standard of care contrary to state law. The appellate court acknowledged that the trial judge did make references to the "prudent tennis player," but held that the prudent person rule was set forth with specificity in the instruction: "When a person, acting in a given set of circumstances, fails to exercise that degree of care for the safety of another which a reasonably prudent person would have exercised in the same or similar circumstances, said person is said to be negligent." Without condoning the lower court's reference to prudent tennis players, the appellate court concluded that it was simply a way of putting the plaintiff's actions in context and that, as a whole, a specialized standard was *not* imposed. The trial judge's charge to the jury was therefore an accurate statement of the law.

The defendant maintained that it was entitled to an instruction to the effect that even though the defendant's duty was to anticipate usual occurrences, it had *no* duty to protect the plaintiff from *remote* events. The appellate court conceded that the particular injury suffered by the plaintiff was unusual. However, the court believed that the defendant misunderstood the essence of foreseeability. (Foreseeability relates to the natural and probable consequences of an act—one need only reasonably foresee that *an* injury may result from a dangerous condition on the premises. The *particular* kind of injury need not have been foreseen.) Moreover, the trial judge specifically stated that, "I do not mean that the defendant had the duty to foresee the unforeseeable."

The appellate court concluded that, where a requested charge is fairly covered by the trial judge's general charge, a specific jury instruction is not required.

The trial judge instructed that, "Proximate cause need not be the sole and only cause. It need not be the last or latter cause. It is a proximate cause if it occurs with another cause which, at the same time, produces the injury." The defendant argued that this explanation of proximate cause was deficient. The appellate court disagreed, explaining that this instruction was consistent with the court's prior holdings that there may be concurring proximate causes that contribute to a plaintiff's injury and that a defendant's negligence is not always rendered remote merely because a second cause intervenes.

The defendant also challenged the trial justice's refusal to give its requested instruction on remote and intervening causes. The defendant's argument appeared to be that the plaintiff had worn an *unusual* ring that caught on the girder and thus was an intervening cause of her injury. The trial judge ruled that the plaintiff's wearing of a ring was not an intervening cause. The defendant argued that that issue should have been submitted to the jury with proper instructions.

In order for an independent intervening cause to replace a defendant's negligence as the proximate cause of an accident, the original negligent conduct must have become totally inoperative as a cause of the injury. There was no question that the plaintiff's ring caught on the girder. However, the defendant's original conduct did not become totally inoperative as a cause of the injury. The wearing of the ring was, at most, a *concurrent* cause that united with the negligence of the defendant, and thus resulted in the particular injury to the plaintiff's finger. The trial judge correctly decided this issue as a matter of law.

Finally, the court considered the defendant's claim that it was entitled to a directed verdict on the grounds that the plaintiff assumed the risk of her injury because she voluntarily climbed the lower girder to get the tennis ball and because she acknowledged that those who climb risk a fall. In deciding whether a plaintiff knows and understands the extent of the risk incurred, the standard is a subjective one. If more than one reasonable inference can be drawn, assumption of the risk is an issue for the jury to decide.

In this case, more than one inference could have been drawn from the plaintiff's conduct. The plaintiff had previously retrieved balls from the girder and had observed other players doing. The jury could draw the inference that the plaintiff perceived, and therefore assumed, *no* risk in her actions.

The defendant's appeal was accordingly denied, and Ms. Hueston walked away with a damaged finger and a check for $75,000 in her pocket. And the tennis club no doubt gladly shelled out $180 to cover up girders that had caused it so much trouble over the years.

Chapter 13

Two-Wheeled Trouble: Establishing Product Liability

Burns v. Cannondale Bicycle Co., 876 P.2d 415 (Utah 1994)

Brian Burns purchased an expensive Cannondale bicycle from The Bicycle Center in Salt Lake City, and a month later, he was riding along when the bike abruptly stopped and threw him over the handle bars.

A few weeks after the accident, Burns retuned the bike to the store for repairs and a determination of what caused it to malfunction. Phillip Blomquist, the owner of the shop, allegedly told Burns, "there was a problem with the brake" and "they had to replace something." However, Blomquist later testified that nothing was wrong with the bicycle and that no part was replaced.

Exactly three years after the accident, Burns filed suit against Cannondale Bicycle Company and The Bicycle Center for breach of the implied warranty of merchantability, breach of certain express warranties, and products liability. He also asserted a claim against The Bicycle Center for negligent assembly.

In his complaint, Burns alleged that the accident was caused when the front brake spring popped off, causing the brakes to clamp down on the front tire. In an attempt to determine the effect of a dislodged spring, Burns consulted an expert who supposedly stated that a dislodged spring would have the *opposite* effect. According to this expert, the loss of the spring would cause the brake pads to release *away* from the tire rim rather than cause the brakes to engage. This opinion was corroborated by the defendants' experts, who testified that such a brake malfunction would *not* cause the bike to stop suddenly.

The defendants subsequently moved for summary judgment, claiming that Burns could not prevail on his claims because he lacked evidence of a defect that could have caused the accident. Burns, admitting that he lacked such evidence, claimed that the existence of such a defect could be "inferred" by the fact finder.

Alleging that the defendants had disposed of the defective part, Burns also argued that the spoliation of evidence established the defect. Burns further claimed that Blomquist's statements constituted an admission of liability, or at the very least created an issue of fact as to whether a causal defect existed. Rejecting Burns's arguments, the trial court granted the defendants' summary judgment, concluding that Burns's inability to prove a specific defect and furnish evidence of causation made Blomquist's alleged admissions immaterial. The court also concluded that Burns failed to establish a factual basis for his spoliation claim. Burns appealed.

Product Liability Requirements

In order to prevail on a claim for strict products liability, the plaintiff must show (1) that the product was unreasonably dangerous due to a defect or defective condition, (2) that the defect existed at the time the product was sold, and (3) that the defective condition was a cause of the plaintiff's injuries.

The fact that someone was injured while using a product does not establish that the product was unreasonably dangerous when put to its intended use. In order to defeat the defendants' motion for summary judgment, Burns had to provide evidence that a defect existed at the time he bought the bicycle and that the defect caused his injury. It was not enough to merely contend that a defect existed, show that an accident occurred, and assume the two were related.

Destruction of Evidence

Burns admitted that he could not prove the existence of a defect, but he claimed that it would properly be inferred if the fact finder determined The Bicycle Center disposed of a part from Burns's bike. Burns based his claim on the doctrine of spoliation of evidence, which holds that when a party fails to provide (or destroys) evidence favorable to the opposing party, the court will assume the evidence's adverse content.

However, even if such a defective part existed and was discarded, the requirements for spoliation in the present case had not been met. Burns had not brought suit for his injuries, nor even notified the defendants that he was considering such action, at the time the part was allegedly discarded. By his own admission, Burns did not even contemplate filing suit at that time, but he only later became interested in litigation after viewing a televised report about the notorious trial attorney Melvin Belli. Thus, the defendants were not even on notice of the impending filing of such an action at the time the part was supposedly discarded.

The Defendant's Statements

Burns also claimed that Blomquist's alleged admissions created an issue of fact precluding summary judgment. The appellate court disagreed. Blomquist allegedly admitted that there was a problem with the bike that required repair. However, Blomquist begged to differ, stating that, after disassembling the brake mechanism, he concluded that there was nothing wrong with the bike's brakes. There was clearly an issue of disputed fact as to what Blomquist said.

However, the appellate court noted that the mere existence of genuine issues of fact does not preclude the entry of summary judgment if those issues are *immaterial* to resolution of the case. When a party fails to make a showing sufficient to establish an element *essential* to that party's case, there is *not* a genuine issue of material fact, since a failure to prove an essential element of the nonmoving party's case renders all other facts immaterial.

Even the most favorable characterization of Blomquist's alleged statements did not constitute the requisite showing for strict products liability. Statements that the bike "malfunctioned" and that "it was the bike's fault" were *not* sufficient to establish the existence of a causal defect. Burns had not provided any evidence as to what the defect was or how it caused his injuries. In fact, Burns's initial allegation that the brake spring came off, thereby causing the brakes to suddenly engage, was *contradicted* by experts on both sides. Burns had simply not met his burden by basing his case on the alleged admissions of Blomquist, which went no further than to recognize there was something wrong with the bike.

In the end, Burns failed to make a sufficient showing that a defect existed and that his injuries were caused thereby, and accordingly, the appellate court affirmed the summary judgment in favor of the defendants. Some impartial observers might chalk the entire incident up to "operator error."

Chapter 14

Backyard Basketball: A Noisy Proposition

Schild v. Rubin, 232 Cal.App.3d 755 (1991)

Two neighbors—who unfortunately happened to also be lawyers—dribbled a lively dispute from a backyard basketball court into a court of law.

Michael and Yifat Rubin sued their neighbors, Kenneth and Gail Schild, seeking an injunction to prohibit the Schilds from playing basketball on their own property. The trial court issued the injunction pursuant to a statute prohibiting willful harassment.

The Rubins resided with their infant child at a residence in Encino, California. The Schilds lived next door with their two children, thirteen-year-old Jonathan and eleven-year-old Deborah. The Schilds had installed in their backyard a small basketball court. The basketball backboard was about sixty feet from a six-foot-high adobe wall, which separated the two properties. The Rubins' residence was at its closest point approximately six feet from the wall. In due course, Michael Rubin complained to the Schilds that the noise created by Jonathan when he played basketball interrupted their child's afternoon naps and interfered with their ability to rest and relax in their home.

According to Rubin, the Schilds played basketball three to five times a week, typically in the afternoon, and those sessions usually lasted from five to thirty minutes. Jonathan Schild usually played alone when he arrived home from school or with his father when he returned home from work.

The Schilds tried to be accommodating, and to muffle the sound, they poured concrete into the hollow steel pole supporting the backboard and then added four inches of foam rubber to the back of the backboard. Rubin admitted the situation was somewhat improved, but he still deemed the noise unacceptable.

Shortly thereafter, Rubin again complained of the noise, and one afternoon he asked Jonathan to stop playing. Kenneth Schild told his son Jonathan that he could continue playing for another ten minutes until dinner was ready. Rubin then furiously demanded that Schild stop his son from playing and procceded to spray the basketball court with water from a garden hose. Rubin admitted that he sprayed the basketball court, but claimed that no one was ever "directly sprayed." Rubin deemed the spraying to be the exercise of his right to abate a "private nuisance." Schild and his son, who were wet, considered the spraying an assault.

The Schilds filed a complaint against Rubin for assault, battery, trespass, nuisance, and intentional infliction of emotional distress, and they sought a permanent injunction. Rubin cross-complained against the Schilds for nuisance and intentional infliction of emotional distress, and he too sought a permanent injunction.

A month later, a second basketball-and-hose-spraying incident occurred. The next day, the Schilds obtained a temporary restraining order against the Rubins. The order was followed by a petition for an injunction prohibiting harassment. The court enjoined the Rubins from "alarming, annoying, or harassing" the Schilds, and ordered that the Rubins "not direct communication of any kind, either oral, telephone, written or otherwise" to the Schilds and "not interfere in any way with the peaceful use and enjoyment of the Schilds' residence, including the full and appropriate use of the basketball play area." Rubin did not appeal the issuance of this injunction.

Several weeks later, Rubin obtained a temporary restraining order against the Schilds under the willful harassment statute. Rubin sought a total ban on basketball play. The court ordered the Schilds "not to engage in any basketball playing except from 11 a.m. to 3:30 p.m. and from 4:30 p.m. to 6:30 p.m. daily."

About a month later, the court held a hearing on Rubin's application for a permanent injunction. After the court reviewed the evidence, it granted Rubin's petition for an injunction prohibiting harassment. In this regard, the court ordered that the Schilds not alarm, annoy, or harass the Rubins and that the Schilds were "not to engage in basketball playing on their property of any kind except between 10:00 a.m. and 12:00 p.m.; between 2:30 p.m. and 5:30 p.m.; and between 7:30 p.m. and 8:30 p.m. daily."

The Schilds appealed.

Harassment Statute

The Rubins characterized the basketball playing as amounting to a nuisance and argued that "nuisance is equivalent to harassment." The court responded that not every activity which is "offensive to the senses and interferes with the comfortable enjoyment of life" constitutes a nuisance. The question, the court said, was not whether the plaintiffs had been annoyed, but whether there had been an injury to their legal rights.

The Schilds contended evidence was lacking to support the requisite elements of the willful harassment statute. The Schilds maintained that the noise from a bouncing ball and the verbal chatter of several people engaged in recreational basketball in a residential backyard, playing at reasonable times of the day for less than thirty minutes at a time and no more than five times per week, did *not* constitute unlawful harassment.

At the heart of the controversy were the related issues of whether the Schilds' conduct "seriously" alarmed, annoyed, or harassed the Rubins to the extent that the conduct "actually caused substantial emotional distress" to the Rubins. The act, unfortunately, did not define the phrase "substantial emotional distress." The court suspected that the bulk of any emotional distress suffered by the Rubins was generated by the litigation itself, rather than the noise from basketball. The record, however, was sufficient to establish, as the Rubins asserted, that the noise penetrated the air, offended "the senses" of the Rubins, invaded their "peace and quiet," and generally interfered with their "comfortable enjoyment of life and property."

Nonetheless, there was *no* medical, psychological, or other evidence that the sounds, however offensive and annoying, caused the Rubins "substantial emotional distress." A reasonable person, the court mused, must realize that complete tranquility is seldom attainable, and some degree of temporary annoyance is the natural consequence of living among others in an urban environment. The court found that the Schilds' basketball playing occurred in a manner that constituted a reasonable use of their property. Accordingly, the Schilds' basketball playing was not so outrageous, extreme, intense, or enduring as to come within the scope of injunctive relief for willful harassment.

The court also noted that Rubin admitted during his argument at trial that, "Basketball playing serves a legitimate purpose. It's exercise. It gets the family together." The Schilds alleged that their basketball playing, done in a reasonable way, reflected a legitimate exercise of their constitutional right to enjoy life, possess property, and pursue happiness and privacy.

The judgment was reversed, and the injunction issued against the Schilds was dissolved. The court failed to mention it, but the moral of the story was clear: if you like to play basketball, it might be best *not* to move next door to a lawyer with a trigger-happy garden hose.

Chapter 15

Body Check: An Intentional Tort?

Hanson v. Kynast, 526 N.E.2d 327 (Ohio 1987)

Brian Hanson, a lacrosse player for Ohio State University, tragically sustained paralyzing injuries while playing in a game against Ashland University. The question was whether he could successfully sue the university and the player who caused his injury.

The facts of the case were fairly straightforward. With some four minutes remaining in the game, Roger Allen, an OSU player, intercepted a pass and scored a goal. As Allen crossed the goal line, he was body-checked from behind by an Ashland defender, William Kynast. This body check caused Allen to fall, and in a show of harassment, Kynast lingered over Allen, taunting him. Then, in a display of support for his downed colleague, Brian Hanson grabbed Kynast from the back and held him in a bear hug. Kynast immediately—almost instinctively—twisted and flipped Hanson upside down, causing Hanson's head to strike the ground.

To recover for his injuries, Hanson filed suit against Kynast and Ashland University. The university filed a motion for summary judgment, which the court granted. The trial court held that no agency relationship existed between Kynast and the university, and that the university did not have a legal duty to have an ambulance at the game. Hanson alleged that the failure of the university to provide timely medical attention contributed to his injury.

The trial court also granted summary judgment to Kynast. The trial court reasoned that Hanson assumed the risk of injury when he grabbed Kynast. The court explained:

> We . . . find from the plaintiff's own testimony that in grabbing the defendant in the manner that he did precipitated and was the cause of his injury. We find that there was no activity on the part of the defendant which would justify the grabbing of the defendant, any more than where the players, in the heat of the moment, become engulfed in fisticuffs when they believe a companion to have been dealt with unfairly, with the fists and arms flaying madly.

Ordinarily, the court pointed out, no cause of action exists when a participant in a sporting event is injured by another participant. However, an athlete is not immune from liability for an intentional tort, and the duty not to commit such a tort remains intact, even in the heat of battle in a body-contact sport such as lacrosse.

The appellate court remarked that if Kynast, minutes after the game was over, had run across the field and thrown a body block at Hanson, then an obvious cause of action would exist. However, the facts presented to the trial court showed no evidence of Kynast's intent to injure Hanson. Everyone agreed (including all three courts that reviewed the case) that Kynast's action was reflexive and instinctive.

The judgment in favor of Kynast was therefore affirmed, leaving Hanson without remedy and reinforcing the observation that the sporting life can be very hazardous indeed.

Part IV

Intellectual Property

Chapter 16

Svelte Swimsuit: A Competitive Business

TYR Sport, Inc. v. Warnaco Swimwear Inc., 709 F. Supp.2d 802 C.D. Calif. (2010)

Both TYR Sport and Warnaco Swimwear (better known as Speedo) design and manufacture high-end swimwear for competitive swimmers. To promote its line, Speedo hired Mark Schubert, who was the head coach for USA Swimming, the national governing body of the sport. With some bitterness, TYR alleged that the relationship between Speedo and Shubert rendered USA Swimming a *de facto* sales agent for Speedo. Litigation between the two swimsuit giants ensured.

TYR specifically alleged that in exchange for payments from Speedo, USA Swimming acted as a promoter for Speedo, and made false statements that Speedo's products were "superior" to those of its rivals. Most notably, Schubert was accused of misleading national team members by claiming that the Speedo suit, the LZR Racer, provided an advantage over the clothing made by Speedo's rivals. USA Swimming also allegedly altered images of sponsored athletes to remove logos of Speedo's competitors.

The accusations did not end there. USA Swimming was said to have refused Speedo's competitors the ability to advertise in the official magazine, to sponsor USA Swimming-sanctioned meets, and to post signs at meets. TYR further alleged that Speedo falsely advertised its products to team dealers, who accounted for a large portion of competitive swimwear sales.

Much of the controversy centered on the run-up to the 2008 Olympic games in Beijing. At the time, high-end swimsuit manufacturers were engaged in something of an arms race. Each was attempting to market suits that could significantly reduce the swimming times of elite swimmers. Speedo released the LZR Racer, and TYR was frantically working to develop its own elite racing suit, the Tracer Rise, in time for the Beijing games.

Schubert earnestly touted the advantages of the LZR Racer. Prior to a swim meet in England, he gathered the swimmers on the national team and encouraged them to wear the suit, boldly claiming that it offered a "two percent advantage." Schubert also allegedly told the swimmers to wear the Speedo suit at trials or "they may end up at home watching the Olympics on NBC."

The Speedo-wearing swimmers experienced unparalleled success at the Olympics. All told, 86 percent of the swimming medals in Beijing, including 91 percent of the gold medals, were won by swimmers wearing the LZR Racer. The arms race continued after the Olympics, but everything came to an abrupt end in July 2009, when the sport's international governing body decided to ban high-performance full-body suits, including the LZR Racer and the Tracer Rise. This effectively ended the market for such swimsuits.

At this stage in the litigation, TYR had seven remaining claims against Speedo, USA Swimming, and Schubert, which consisted primarily of federal and state antitrust claims. TYR also sought an injunction against the defendants.

Federal and State Antitrust Claims

TYR alleged that a conspiracy existed among Speedo, USA Swimming, and Schubert to restrain trade by having USA Swimming act as a *de facto* sales agent for Speedo to the detriment of Speedo's competitors. To succeed, TYR had to prove actual coercion—that USA Swimming and Schubert set a standard, along with the threat of punishing market participants for deviating from that standard. In other words, there can be no restraint of trade without a *restraint*. Promotion and persuasion are not actionable as antitrust violations, even where the speaker holds extraordinary prestige and influence. Such speech is just part of the friendly warfare of business competition.

With these principles in mind, the court turned to TYR's evidence that Speedo, USA Swimming, and Schubert coerced elite swimmers to wear Speedo suits as opposed to those of its competitors.

The Olympics Comment. The court identified a single allegation that potentially presented the necessary coercive conduct. Schubert was quoted as saying, "I would strongly advise the swimmers to wear the Speedo suit at trials, or they may end up at home watching the Olympics on NBC." The court recognized that this statement could be interpreted in two ways: (1) a swimmer wearing a non-Speedo suit would be at a competitive disadvantage, thereby risking a loss at the trials, or (2) Schubert would exclude a swimmer from the Olympic Team if the swimmer chose to wear a non-Speedo suit.

The defendants presented evidence that Schubert's statement could not possibly be interpreted as a threat because Schubert lacked the authority to exclude swimmers from the Olympic team. The burden then fell to TYR to produce evidence rebutting the defendants' showing, and TYR conceded that it could not do so. The court also noted that the actual selection of the open water team belied TYR's claim of coercion—the swimmers chosen to represent the United States wore TYR suits.

Schubert's Attempts to Persuade Elite Swimmers. TYR argued that Schubert restrained trade by attempting to persuade several elite swimmers to wear Speedo suits from his position of "extraordinary influence." However, the court pointed out that statements from a position of influence alone do not constitute "restraints." A person or organization having prestige or respect does not lose the right to promote or criticize products in the marketplace. A statement must set some standard backed by a threat to punish to be actionable as an antitrust violation.

In the court's view, Schubert's statement to swimmers that the Speedo suit was "faster" was *not* a restraint on trade. Schubert did not threaten to take any action against them if they chose not to wear Speedo, and no action was taken when a swimmer chose the competition. Schubert's comment was simply a promotion of Speedo's product, which Schubert was entitled to make, regardless of how influential he was within the swimming community.

Research Collaboration. TYR also argued that Speedo, USA Swimming, and Schubert restrained trade by collaborating to develop faster swimwear, to the exclusion of Speedo's competitors. TYR cited no authority that such collaboration violated antitrust laws. A joint research venture alone does not violate the antitrust laws. This is particularly so where one of the collaborators, USA Swimming, is not even a market participant. TYR pointed to no anti-competitive effect of the joint research project (and in fact, such joint research was likely to have many pro-competitive effects).

Schubert's Role as Technical Advisor. Finally, TYR complained of Schubert's role within USA Swimming to disseminate technical information to the public. TYR argued that as a "gate-keeper," Schubert only disseminated information favorable to Speedo, misstated information, and withheld information favorable to Speedo's competitors. These complaints, the court said, did *not* constitute a restraint of trade because the antitrust laws do not require an ostensibly neutral party to praise competitors equally or to refrain from disparaging a competitor.

When all was said and done, the court denied TYR's request for an injunction, freeing Speedo to pursue its aggressive marketing strategies, shall we say, full "speed."

Chapter 17

All in a Name: Protecting the Ironman Brand

World Triathalon Corp. v. Dunbar, 539 F. Supp. 2d 1270 (D. Hawaii 2008)

As everyone knows, the Ironman Triathlon has grown to become an extremely prominent event. Its owner, World Triathlon Corp. (WTC), owns over 350 trademark registrations, and along with its myriad licensees, it sells a wide array of products featuring the Ironman mark around the world.

The original Ironman triathlon started in 1978. In 1980, Valerie Silk and her husband Henry Grundman agreed to take over the race, and they incorporated Hawaiian Triathlon Corporation (HTC). In 1981, Silk and Grundman moved the race from Oahu to Kailua-Kona and began to secure federal registrations for the Ironman trademarks. In 1989, WTC purchased HTC. As a result of that transaction, several of the participants in the original Ironman race sued HTC and Silk to prevent the sale.

These plaintiffs asked, among other things, that the court enter a preliminary injunction to prevent the sale. The plaintiffs argued that *they* owned the Ironman and that any prior assignment of rights to the Ironman should be set aside as fraudulent. In 1993, the court granted summary judgment in favor of WTC. In spite of that decision, John Dunbar and others organized an Ironman triathlon on Maui from 1994 to 1998, sold Ironman trophies, registered two trademarks and a service mark for "Ironman Triathlon" with the Hawaii Department of Commerce and Consumer Affairs, and lastly, contacted the plaintiffs' licensees, informing those companies that they, not WTC, owned the rights relating to the Ironman.

In 2005, WTC filed suit against Dunbar, alleging violation of the Lanham Trademark Act, common law unfair competition, tortious interference with business relations, and slander of title. The court granted WTC's motion for summary judgment as to its Lanham Act and common law unfair competition claims. The court found that the defendant had known since at least 1993 that he possessed no ownership rights in the Ironman marks. The court further granted the plaintiff's request for declaratory relief that "WTC has superior and exclusive rights to the Ironman marks and the defendant had no ownership or other rights in the Ironman marks." The court noted that in exceptional cases it may award reasonable attorney fees to the prevailing party, and in the present case, it did so.

Trademark Infringement

The court concluded that the defendant's infringement was *not* a close case. In granting the plaintiff's motion for summary judgment on its Lanham Act claim, the court found that there was *no* genuine issue of material fact that the plaintiff owned the Ironman marks, that these marks were incontestable, and that the defendant's actions created a likelihood of confusion. Indeed, the defendant used an identical mark and advertised trophies with this mark in the same publications that the plaintiff used to advertise its events.

Furthermore, the history of the parties revealed that the defendant knew he had no right to use the plaintiff's marks. In 1989, the defendant had sued the plaintiff's predecessor to prevent the sale of HTC to WTC, in part based on the assertion that he owned rights to the Ironman. In 1993, the court granted summary judgment in favor of the defendant.

In other words, the defendant's previous legal action seeking rights relating to the Ironman failed. Therefore, the defendant had known since at least 1993 that he had no ownership rights in the Ironman race or any related trademarks. Despite this knowledge, the defendant (1) organized an Ironman-length triathlon on Maui from 1994 to 1998, (2) sold Ironman trophies through sports catalogs and at the Ironman race itself, (3) registered two trademarks and a service mark for "Ironman Triathlon" with the Hawaiian authorities, and (4) contacted the plaintiff's licensees, informing those companies that he owned the rights to the Ironman.

None of the defendant's arguments persuaded the court that he did not deliberately infringe the plaintiff's trademarks. The defendant argued that (1) he believed he owned the Ironman mark, given their creation of the event, (2) he was convinced that the issue of who owned the Ironman mark had not been determined by the previous case, and (3) he did not "exactly" duplicate the plaintiff's trademark. Each of these arguments, the court said, was either meritless in light of the previous case or unsubstantiated by the facts.

First, the defendant's argument that he acted on a good faith belief that he owned the Ironman event could not be sustained. The defendant had no basis for believing that he had any ownership rights in the Ironman, nor did the defendant establish any good faith belief of non-infringement on the basis that he relied on an opinion of counsel. (The court recognized that in some instances, a good faith belief of non-infringement can be shown through the fact that a defendant received counsel's advice. But the defendant had not revealed any opinion of counsel concerning the Ironman trademarks.)

The court also rejected the defendant's argument that his infringement was not deliberate because there were differences between the plaintiff's Ironman mark and the defendant's use of the word Ironman. The court explained that the defendant was using an *identical* mark to take commercial advantage of the plaintiff's trademarks.

Even viewing all of the evidence in a light most favorable to them, the court found that the defendant failed to raise a genuine issue of material fact in support of any of his defenses. On his senior rights defense (which required a showing of continuous use), the defendant "utterly failed" to meet his burden and produced evidence of only "sporadic use" of the Ironman mark since 1980.

Attorneys' Fees

The court recognized that an award of attorneys' fees pursuant to federal statute was "never automatic and may be limited by equitable considerations." The court noted that the defendant's acts were not limited to selling a few trophies and shirts. Rather, the defendant contacted the plaintiff's licensees and claimed to be the true owner of the Ironman. The court concluded that the defendant deliberately infringed the plaintiff's trademarks, which warranted attorneys' fees. For these reasons, the court awarded the plaintiff attorneys' fees in the amount of $161,147.05.

The defendant contended that his use of the trademark did not rise to the level of willful or deliberate, because he believed he owned the mark. The court disagreed, finding that the defendant knew of the existence of the plaintiff's marks and then deliberately infringed on those marks to sell various products. The defendant had no valid defenses for the infringement. Taken together, these circumstances justified an award of legal fees.

In the end, the plaintiff prevailed, having used strong-arm tactics that befitted an Ironman triathlete.

Chapter 18

Are You Thirsty?: The Sport Drink Wars

Sands, Taylor & Wood Co. v. Quaker Oats Co., 34 F.3d 1340 (7th Cir. 1994)

Who would have thought that the simple words "thirst" and "aid" could cause such consternation.

Sands, Taylor & Wood Company (STW) is a small, Vermont-based company that in 1973 acquired Joseph Middleby, Jr., Inc., a manufacturer of soft drinks. As a result of this acquisition, STW became the owner of trademarks registered to Middleby in 1950 for "THIRST-AID" and "First Aid for Your Thirst."

In August of 1983, Quaker Oats purchased the rights to manufacture the athletic drink Gatorade. Shortly thereafter, Quaker solicited proposals for a new advertising campaign, and one of the candidates was the slogan *Gatorade is Thirst Aid for That Deep Down Body Thirst.* The proposed Thirst Aid campaign was submitted to the legal department for approval, and Quaker's in-house counsel concluded that the words Thirst Aid did not raise any trademark problems because they were used to describe an attribute of the product, rather than as a designation of source or affiliation. At the time, Quaker's legal department did not conduct a trademark search for the term.

On May 12, 1984, the first "Gatorade is Thirst Aid" commercials ran on television. Two weeks later, STW informed Quaker that it was infringing its trademark, to which Quaker's in-house counsel responded that there was no infringement because Quaker was using the words *descriptively.*

STW filed suit a week later, alleging that the Gatorade slogan infringed its registrations and constituted unfair competition under the Lanham Act, state common law, and various state statutes. The court eventually concluded that Quaker *had* infringed STW's trademark, and it awarded STW 10 percent of Quaker's pre-tax profits on Gatorade for the period during which Quaker used "Thirst Aid" in its advertising. The court also awarded STW attorney's fees and costs as well as prejudgment interest. The court entered judgment for STW in the amount of $42,629,399, including prejudgment interest and attorney's fees. The court also permanently enjoined Quaker from using the words "Thirst Aid."

Not surprisingly, Quaker appealed.

Descriptive or Suggestive

The district court granted summary judgment in favor of STW on Quaker's defense that it had made a "fair use" of the phrase *Thirst Aid.* The fair use doctrine is based upon the principle that no one should be able to appropriate descriptive language through trademark registration. To prevail on a fair use defense, the defendant must establish that its use of a registered term is "otherwise than as a trade or service mark," that the term is "descriptive of" the defendant's goods or services, and that the defendant is using the term "fairly and in good faith only to describe to users" those goods and services.

The district court ultimately found that the term *Thirst Aid* was *not* descriptive of Gatorade, but rather was *suggestive*. The court also found that even if the term was descriptive, Quaker could not prevail on the fair use defense because it had used the term as a trademark in its ads. Quaker strongly challenged both of these conclusions.

The district court described the difference between a suggestive mark and a descriptive one as follows: "If the mark imparts information directly, it is descriptive. If it stands for an idea which requires some operation of the imagination to connect it with the goods, it is suggestive." Purporting to apply this test, the district court found that Thirst Aid was suggestive rather than descriptive because it "required imagination to create the impression of an isotonic beverage." Quaker argued that the district court misapplied the relevant legal standard.

As it turned out, the appellate court agreed. The district court thought that in order to be descriptive the term had to bring to mind the product in question—in other words, "create the impression of an isotonic beverage." However, the appellate court held that it was not necessary that a descriptive term depict the product itself, but only that the term refer to a characteristic of the product. Under that test, the district court's conclusion that Thirst Aid was not, as a matter of law, descriptive of Gatorade could *not* stand. In support of its opposition to STW's motion for summary judgment, Quaker presented evidence that consumers understood the words "Thirst Aid" to convey the message that Gatorade helps quench thirst—that is, that the term described a characteristic of Gatorade.

Therefore, the appellate court held that the district court erred in finding "Thirst Aid" suggestive as a matter of law.

"Thirst Aid" as a Trademark

The district court also found that even if "Thirst Aid" was descriptive, Quaker could not prevail on its fair use defense because it used the term as a trademark. A word or phrase functions as a trademark when it is "used by a source of a product to identify itself to the public as the source of its product and to create in the public consciousness an awareness of the uniqueness of the source and of its products."

The district court noted that the term "Thirst Aid" was the most prominent feature of some of the defendant's advertising. Each of the ads included the statement *Gatorade is THIRST AID*. The court therefore found that the way in which the defendant used the term created an impression that the slogan was uniquely associated with Gatorade.

Quaker argued that its use of a descriptive mark in conjunction with its own clearly established trademark, "Gatorade," could not be a trademark use. In support of this argument, Quaker relied in part on this court's prior observation that descriptive terms are "unlikely" to function as trademarks.

The appellate court held that evidence of Quaker's advertisements supported the district court's conclusion that Quaker used *Thirst Aid* as a trademark. Quaker's ads did not simply use the words "Thirst Aid" in a sentence describing Gatorade, but as an "attention-getting symbol." In many of the ads, the words "Thirst Aid" appear more prominently and in larger type than did the word "Gatorade." Further, given the rhyming quality of "Gatorade" and "Thirst Aid," the association between the two terms created by Quaker's ads was likely to be very strong, so that *Thirst Aid* appeared as part of a memorable slogan that was uniquely associated with Quaker's product. Quaker presented no evidence that its ads did not have this effect on consumers.

As a result, the district court did *not* err in concluding that Quaker used *Thirst Aid* as a trademark.

The Question of Abandonment

Because trademark rights are sustained from the use of a mark in commerce and not from mere registration, the owner of a mark will lose his exclusive rights if he fails to use it. A mark is deemed to be thus abandoned when "its use has been discontinued with intent not to resume such use." Two years of nonuse typically creates a prima facie case of abandonment, which may be rebutted by evidence explaining the nonuse or demonstrating the lack of an intent not to resume use.

Quaker contended that STW had no registration rights covering the use of THIRST-AID on a beverage, because the trademark THIRST-AID "First Aid for Your Thirst," the only mark registered for use on beverages (as opposed to beverage syrups), had not been used since 1949. The court rejected this argument.

In the view of the court, the fact that STW and its predecessors had not used the entire slogan THIRST-AID "First Aid for Your Thirst" since 1949 did not necessarily mean that the registration had been abandoned.

Likelihood of Confusion

STW relied not on classic "forward confusion," but on the doctrine of "reverse confusion." Reverse confusion occurs when a large junior user saturates the market with a trademark similar to that of a smaller senior user. In such a case, the junior user does not seek to profit from the goodwill associated with the senior user's mark. Nonetheless, the senior user is injured because the public comes to assume that the senior user's products are really the junior user's, or that the former has become somehow connected to the latter. The result is that the senior user loses the value of the trademark—its product identity, corporate identity, control over its goodwill and reputation, and ability to move into new markets.

Quaker contended, first, that the district court erred in finding a likelihood of confusion because it failed to consider the strength of STW's mark. According to Quaker, the "extensive" use of the words "thirst aid" on other products established the weakness of the plaintiff's marks and weighed heavily against a finding of likelihood of confusion.

The Seventh Circuit court disagreed. Here, both the marks and the goods—Quaker's Gatorade and the isotonic beverage that STW would market but for Quaker's actions—were virtually identical. The court noted that it may make more sense to consider the strength of the mark in terms of its association with the junior user's goods. In this case, there was abundant evidence that consumers strongly associated the word "thirst aid" with Gatorade, even when those words appeared on a product label with a different brand name. It was precisely the strong association between Gatorade and Thirst Aid created by Quaker's ads that was likely to create confusion in this case. Under the circumstances, linking the plaintiff's mark with the defendant's brand name was an aggravation, not a justification.

The Seventh Circuit agreed that the district court's analysis of the trademark infringement factors was sufficient to support its finding that there was a likelihood of confusion and, therefore, infringement. Gatorade would therefore be forced to find another snappy advertising slogan that did not use the dreaded words *thirst* or *aid*.

Chapter 19

Trademark Protection: Distinguishing Matters of Parody

Nike, Inc. v. Just Did It Enterprises, 799 F. Supp. 894 (N.D. Ill. 1992)

An artist named Mike Stanard thought he would do something clever: his company, "Just Did It" Enterprises, manufactured and sold T-shirts and sweatshirts bearing the logo *Mike*, displayed in the same typeset and along with a reproduction of the "swoosh" stripe for which the sports giant Nike has been granted trademark protection.

Nike filed suit against Stanard, alleging trademark infringement, unfair competition, trademark dilution, and deceptive trade practices. Nike also contended that the defendant's use of the trade name "Just Did It" constituted infringement on Nike's slogan "Just Do It."

The parties agreed about the material facts of the case, but disagreed about the legal consequences of Stanard's actions. Nike argued that Stanard's activities constituted trademark infringement and unfair competition, and the company sought injunctive relief as well as attorneys' fees. Stanard countered that his work was protected as a parody, and that Nike was not entitled to any relief.

Nike sought an order that Stanard had infringed the company's exclusive rights in the trademark *Nike*, the swoosh-stripe design, the *Nike*-and-swoosh-design combination, and the trademark slogan "Just Do It." Nike sought a permanent injunction enjoining the defendant from further use of the Nike trademarks. Nike also sought the following relief: (1) an order pursuant to the Federal Trademark Act that required Stanard to deliver for destruction all infringing articles, (2) an order requiring Stanard to account for and pay Nike for all profits he had realized from the infringing activity, and (3) an order requiring Stanard to pay the costs of this action and reasonable attorneys' fees.

In order to obtain an injunction, Nike had to establish the following: (1) that it will succeed or has succeeded on the merits, (2) no adequate remedy at law exists, (3) irreparable harm will arise absent injunctive relief, (4) the irreparable harm that Nike will suffer in absence of injunctive relief outweighs the irreparable harm Stanard will suffer if the injunction is granted, and (5) the injunction will not harm the public interest.

Success on the Merits

In order to establish liability for trademark infringement and unfair competition, Nike had to show: (1) that it had a protectable trademark and (2) the likelihood of confusion as to the source or origin of Stanard's product. Nike clearly established that it had a protectable trademark. The trademark NIKE, the swoosh stripe design, and the trademark NIKE alongside the swoosh stripe were registered trademarks. The company's registration provided prima facie evidence of their validity as trademarks and of Nike's exclusive right to use the marks on apparel and related accessories. Moreover, each of these registrations became incontestable under the

Federal Trademark Act, and accordingly constituted conclusive evidence of their distinctiveness as trademarks.

Although not registered, the slogan "Just Do It" was also entitled to trademark protection. An unregistered mark is still entitled to trademark protection when its use is inherently distinctive as applied to the goods on which it is used, or when its use has acquired secondary meaning in the marketplace. Although Stanard was correct in arguing that "Just Do It" is a common phrase used in the English language, Nike's extensive use of the phrase in association with apparel rendered it so distinctive that it was entitled to trademark protection. Therefore, the court concluded as a matter of law that Nike had established the validity of the marks in question.

Next, the court evaluated the likelihood of confusion resulting from Stanard's use of MIKE with the swoosh stripe. Seven factors were analyzed in determining the likelihood of confusion:

- The degree of similarity between the marks in appearance and suggestion,
- The similarity of the products for which the name was used,
- The area and manner of concurrent use,
- The degree of care likely to be exercised by consumers,
- The strength of the complainant's mark,
- Actual confusion, and
- An intent on the part of the alleged infringer to palm off his products as those of another.

Evaluating these factors, the court found that there was a significant likelihood of confusion resulting from Stanard's use of a mark similar to Nike's. A comparison of the parties' marks revealed that they were virtually identical. In fact, the only difference was that Stanard had substituted an "M" for an "N." Even Stanard admitted that from a distance, the two marks could *not* be distinguished.

Nike's marks were worthy of strong protection. Each of the marks had been used extensively in Nike's promotion and advertising, and it was undisputed that the marks were widely recognized and associated with the company. Moreover, the incontestable status of Nike's federal registrations was evidence of the strength of the marks.

Evidence was submitted that indicated that Stanard intended to pass off his merchandise as that of Nike. Stanard admitted to having actual knowledge of Nike's trademark rights, as well as a desire to benefit from Nike's advertising and promotion. When asked whether someone reading his T-shirt from across the room may think that it said Nike, Stanard responded. "That's the whole point."

Evidence of *actual* consumer confusion is not required for *likelihood* of confusion to be established, but Stanard admitted that actual confusion could easily occur if his products were viewed from a distance. The court found that Nike sufficiently demonstrated likelihood of confusion and thus trademark infringement.

Stanard argued that his work was entitled to protection under the First Amendment as a parody. The court explained that parody is not a defense to trademark infringement, but rather is a factor in determining the likelihood of confusion. Additionally, a defendant's parody argument will be disregarded where the purpose of the similarity is to capitalize on the popularity of the famous mark for the defendant's project.

In a previous case cited by the court, the defendant designed a logo displaying the words "Mutant of Omaha" and an emaciated human face wearing a warbonnet. This design was placed on T-shirts in conjunction with the phrase "Nuclear Holocaust Insurance." The reverse side of the T-shirts read, "When the world's in ashes, we'll have you covered." The defendant also designed a shirt reading "Mutant of Omaha's Wild Kingdom," featuring a one-eyed tiger. Not amused, Mutual of Omaha filed a lawsuit claiming that the defendant's design infringed on their trademark. In finding trademark infringement, the court rejected the defendant's claim of parody, finding that the defendant's logo did not create a clear distinction as to the source of the message and did not dispel the likelihood of confusion.

In another case cited by the court, the defendant designed T-shirts bearing the logo "Hard Rain Café." The defendant claimed that this was a parody, poking fun at the constant rain in Seattle. The court also rejected that argument, finding that the logo designs were so similar that consumer confusion was likely.

In the present case, the court found that the circumstances were similar and that the defendant's use of the *Mike* logo and swoosh stripe created a likelihood of confusion that constituted infringement and unfair competition.

Other Factors

The balancing of hardships clearly favored Nike. The company had invested a great deal of expense in advertising and promoting its trademarks Nike, swoosh stripe, and "Just Do It," thus making them the strong, famous, and valuable marks that they have become. Nike had no control over the quality of the garments to which Stanard affixed the *Mike* logo. Given that the two marks were confusing, it was possible that consumers might attribute any defects in a *Mike* garment to Nike, thus further damaging the company's reputation.

Because the court found that Nike prevailed on the merits, that Nike would suffer irreparable harm should an injunction not be granted, and that the balancing of harm decidedly favored Nike, the court granted a permanent injunction preventing the defendant from infringing on any Nike trademark in any manner. The court also ordered the defendant to deliver any remaining merchandise, advertisements, or any other material bearing the MIKE logo.

Attorneys' Fees

The Federal Trademark Act provides that in exceptional cases of trademark infringement, the prevailing party is entitled to reasonable attorneys' fees, absent extenuating circumstances. The "exceptional case" requirement can be fulfilled when the defendant's infringing acts were willful and intentional.

In this case, Stanard willfully and knowingly designed his product to infringe on Nike's trademark. He purposely designed his shirts to resemble Nike products, using the same typeset and trademark swoosh stripe as Nike's merchandise. Stanard named his company "Just Did It" Enterprises in order to further identify his product with Nike's. Moreover, Stanard's own solicitation letter revealed that he knew his activity constituted infringement: "As you might imagine, this is probably going to be a VERY LIMITED OFFER!"

Despite Nike's objections, Stanard continued his infringing activity. The court found that Stanard's willful infringement qualified this as an exceptional case, warranting the imposition of attorneys' fees.

All in all, the whole episode was a very expensive foray into the trademark infringement world by a guy, with a funny idea, named Mike.

Chapter 20

Consumer Confusion: Issues of Infringement

Nautilus Group v. ICON Health and Fitness,
372 F.3d 1330 (Fed. Cir. 2004)

Nautilus and ICON were direct competitors in the market for home exercise equipment. Both companies produced resistance training systems that used bendable rods. In the Nautilus product, called the Bowflex, the rods were arranged vertically. When a user pulled on a cable connected to the upper ends of the rods, the rods *bowed* outward. Nautilus started producing the Bowflex in 1984, registered the trademark for the Bowflex brand in 1986, and held two patents on related technology.

Since 1993, when Nautilus began to directly market its Bowflex exerciser to consumers, the company had invested over $233 million in promotion efforts. Nautilus's advertising focused on infomercials, the Internet, and print publications. As a result, over 780,000 machines were sold, with total revenues of $900 million.

In 2002, the company ICON introduced a competing rod-based resistance training system that it called CrossBow. Its bendable rods were arranged horizontally so that they bent downward rather than outward. According to ICON, the product's resemblance to a medieval crossbow inspired the name. In ICON's two-line logo for the machine, the "o" in "Cross" was replaced by a circular crosshairs. Beneath the mark, in smaller type, appeared an additional line, "by Weider," identifying the machine's source. ICON had spent $13 million on marketing in many of the same advertising channels as Nautilus.

Nautilus filed a suit for trademark infringement, and later a preliminary injunction, to suspend ICON's use of the Cross-Bow trademark. The district court determined that Nautilus had established likelihood of confusion between the marks such that irreparable injury could be presumed, and a preliminary injunction was granted.

The core element of trademark infringement is whether the reasonably prudent consumer is likely to be confused as to the origin of the good or service bearing one of the marks. A district court may grant a preliminary injunction when the plaintiff demonstrates either (1) a combination of probable success on the merits and the possibility of irreparable injury, or (2) the existence of serious questions about the merits and the balance of hardships weigh heavily in the plaintiff's favor.

Probable success on the merits requires a showing that the similarity of the marks, among other factors, has created a likelihood of confusion as to the source or origin of the goods. If a likelihood of confusion between the marks is found, irreparable injury to the plaintiff may be presumed.

The District Court Decision

The district court closely examined the following factors that constitute trademark infringement:

Similarity of Marks and Products. The district court began its analysis by considering the similarity of the marks and their associated products. The court observed that, aside from the shared use of the word "bow," the marks' respective appearances and meanings were dissimilar. On the other hand, the competing products were virtually interchangeable. Because the close similarity in the products was likely to create confusion, the district court reasoned that less similarity between the marks was necessary. The court determined that Nautilus prevailed on similarity of marks and relatedness of goods.

Strength of the Mark. Although the district court did not view Bowflex as a particularly creative mark, it found that Nautilus had invested significantly in the brand name, so that it was now broadly recognized. For this reason, the district court determined that strength of the mark was a factor in Nautilus's favor.

Similarity of Marketing Channels. The court found that similarity of marketing channels also weighed in favor of Nautilus. Both companies utilized identical marketing channels (including infomercials, print ads, and the Internet) to promote their products.

Actual Confusion. Nautilus sought to establish actual confusion by presenting evidence of several telephone calls to its sales center from customers interested in ICON's product. The suggestion of any actual confusion was, in the court's view, sufficient to confirm the possibility of future confusion. From this circumstantial evidence, the court speculated that this potential confusion might have been intentionally created by ICON: "By naming its product CrossBow, the defendant invited comparison and reference to the Bowflex." In the court's opinion, ICON had unfairly capitalized on Nautilus's successful marketing of "bow" in the context of exercise equipment. Intent to confuse was a factor that was found *against* ICON.

Care in Purchasing. The degree of care in purchasing was the *only* factor that, in the court's opinion, supported ICON. Because the Nautilus and ICON machines varied widely in price, the district court reasoned that it would be fair to expect that customers would carefully investigate the range of available products before purchasing. The court concluded that this high degree of care in purchasing would minimize the possibility that consumers would mistakenly buy a CrossBow, thinking that it was a Bowflex.

Weighing all the factors, the court determined therefore that a likelihood of confusion existed between the Bowflex and Cross-Bow marks. The marks were somewhat similar, and there was evidence of actual confusion. Moreover, Bowflex was a strong mark, and there was circumstantial evidence that CrossBow chose its name to take advantage of Bowflex's popularity. Although consumers might be likely to take some care in buying an exercise machine, the possibility of confusion was increased because of the use of the same advertising channels and the similarity of the products. Analysis of the factors favored Bowflex, and they demonstrated the plaintiff's probable success on the merits.

The Appeal

On appeal, ICON made several arguments in favor of vacating the preliminary injunction. The company's primary focus was on the findings made by the district court with respect to its alleged intent to confuse, evidence of actual confusion, the strength of the Bowflex mark, and the similarity between the two marks.

The appellate court disagreed that the district court's balancing was clearly erroneous or an incorrect application of the law. Because the marks shared the term "bow," they were at least somewhat similar. ICON took the view that because "bow" is a common term, any comparison of the marks should focus more on the distinctive "flex" and "cross" components.

Setting aside the intent to confuse and evidence of actual confusion factors, there remained sufficient evidence to justify the preliminary injunction in Nautilus's favor. The degree of similarity of the marks, proximity of the products and services, strength of the Bowflex mark, and similarity of marketing channels are all factors that the court found to favor Nautilus.

As for the similarity of the marks, the court stated that the marks were not that similar, but recognized that this weakness was to some extent compensated for by the identity of the products and the strength of Nautilus's mark. In the end, the court was not prepared to say that the district court abused its discretion in finding likelihood of confusion and issuing a preliminary injunction in favor of Nautilus.

To put it in common vernacular, the Bowflex flexed its muscles and the CrossBow, well, it had to bow out.

Index

Index

Index

Index

Miniature trampolines, 53

Mutual of Omaha, 118

N

Narragansett Tennis Club, x, 73

Nautilus Group, 123–124

Nautilus Group v. ICON Health and Fitness, 372 F.3d 1330 (2004), 123

Negligence, 10, 22, 29, 51, 76

New Orleans City Park, xi, 43–44

New Orleans City Park Improvement Association, 43

New York Health & Racquet Club, xi, 19

Nike, xi, 115–116

Nike v. Just Did It Enterprises, 799 F. Supp. 894 (1992), 115

Notice of expulsion, 66–67

Nudity, 59–60

Nuernberger, Steven, 63–64

O

Ohio State University, 91

Out-of possession landlords, 21, 30–31

P

Pappalardo, Michael, xi, 19–20

Pappalardo v. New York Health & Racquet Club, 279 A.D.2d 134 (2000), 19

Parks, Harry, 63–64

Parody, 115

Partnership agreements, 66–68

"Pec dec" chest-press machine, x, 29

Premises liability, 29

Pritikin Longevity Center and Spa, ix, 13

Product liability, 79

Product liability requirements, 80–82

Proximate cause, 76

Prudent person rule, 75

Q

Quaker Oats Co., 107–108

R

Release clause, 8

Release of negligence, 8–9

Rental agreements, 29, 30

Reverse confusion, 111

Richter, Dearmedia, 55–56

Richter v. Limax International, Inc., 45 F.3d 1464 (1995), 53

Rubin, Michael, 85–86

Rubin, Yifat, 85–86

Index

Trademark infringement
  cases involving, xi, 102–104,
    108–109
  establishing liability for, 116
  factors that constitute,
    124–126
  issues, 123
Trademark protection, 115
Trademarks, 110–111
Treadmills, ix, 6–7
Tringali, Alessio, 33–34, 36–38, 38,
    39–40
Tringali, Lenora, 37
Trotter, Arna, 64
TYR Sports, Inc., x, 95–96
TYR Sports, Inc. v. Warnaco
    Swimwear Inc., 709 F.
    Supp.2d 802 (2010), 95

U

University of Dayton, x, 25
USA Swimming, x, 95, 96
U. S. Court of Appeals for the
    Tenth Circuit, 55, 56

U.S. Fire Insurance Company, 49

W

Warnaco Swimwear Inc., 95
Weights, x, 25–26
Weil, Max Harry, 35
Windows, xi, 19–20
Wooderson v. Ortho
    Pharmaceutical Corp.,
    235 Kan. 387 (1984), 55
World Triathalon Corp. v. Dunbar,
    539 F.Supp.2d 1270
    (2008), 101
World Triathlon Corp. (WTC), 101–
    102, 102
WTC. *See* World Triathlon Corp.
    (WTC)

Z

Zipusch v. LA Workout, 155 Cal.
    App.4th 1281 (2007), 5
Zipusch, Yoko, ix

134

About the Author

Cecil C. Kuhne III is a litigator in the Dallas office of Fulbright & Jaworski L.L.P. He once joined a more upscale health club, reasoning that the financial commitment would motivate him to go more often. When he later calculated that each workout session was costing $300, he quietly let his membership lapse.